N.R. Adams

Sensum

Untangling Our Innermost Interpretations

A Context Narrative

About Coming to Our Senses

Published by IngramSpark June 15, 2020
ISBN: 978-0-578-68390-4 (paperback)

Dedication

To my oldest child, with your keen intelligence, affection, and continuing state of grace, you have a way of clearing crud when it is murky, and you make it more fun when it is sunny.

To my middle one, with your powerful spirit and your incredible creativity and melodies, you encourage me with ardent words and chirpy laughter and keep me going.

To my youngest, with your tender heart, piercing intellect, and comforting conversations, you make gray days lighthearted and have a way of diffusing even the gloomiest moments.

And all three of you keep me straightened out.

Acknowledgments

I want to thank my brave, warmhearted mother, Dafina, who showed me strength and unconditional love.

I would like to acknowledge my extended family for your loving involvement in our lives. Your affections and care will forever be in my heart.

I would also like to thank Sandy, Jim, Jason, Maeve, Camie, Elise, and the awesome Hunter family in Crestline. Your outlook on life, and your sense of humor and insightful honesty are irreplaceable. You have left invaluable impressions on me and helped to light my way.

Table of Contents

"Ideally, what should be said to every child, repeatedly, throughout his or her school life is something like this: 'You are in the process of being indoctrinated. We have not yet evolved a system of education that is not a system of indoctrination. We are sorry, but it is the best we can do."

– Doris Lessing, *The Golden Notebook*

There are countless books written about world society by analysts and professional writers with seemingly endless explanations, clever references, and questionable agendas. We have television shows, expert panels, and never-ending debates. It's like being stuck in a hamster-wheel, and, unless one chooses to hide from the world, one can't seem to escape.

Does an addict need hundreds of pages of scientific interpretations of what alcohol does on a cellular level, or do they need to face themselves? These choices might involve a lifetime of struggles—or one lucid moment—and our entire society will, in some form, benefit from that one small ripple.

We can no longer say, "I didn't know," but we *can* be honest in claiming we hand-picked what we *wanted* to hear.

Be this as it may, what I have to say is plain. Sometimes it is inappropriate, occasionally laughable, and at times devastating—just like real life. The main self-serving agenda I have is the hunger and the will to live in a less selfish, less muddled, and less violent world.

I would imagine that most of us don't wake up in the morning with plans of perpetuating more confusion about ideas and beliefs around the globe. In the interest of this aforementioned hope, what I have here is a list of social and verbal clarifications—simple, short, and one page at a time.

"If you are out to describe the truth,
leave elegance to the tailor."
– Ludwig Boltzmann

The Birth and the Snowballing of Complication

In some ways, humanity has made leaps. In other ways, little has changed. We like to believe that refining our social manners can alter who we are on the inside.

But, while polishing our surface to make us more presentable, our coat might shine, but the inside dirt remains. Too afraid to look in the mirror, we run for the door, while poverty, abuse, and war, are still rampant all over the world.

We have better teeth, indoor plumbing, and tiresome *informed* and *appropriate* conversations with little or no resolve. We are still at the mercy of those who are hollow inside, obsessed with external powers that come through controlling others, ignorant of the real power of forgiveness, genuine understanding, and grace.

But we *do* have a choice. We *can* say, "I've had enough." Enough lying to ourselves about our shortcomings, as these types of flaws blanket everything we believe and choose to do. Enough misinterpretations of books and words, so we can oppress others. This paranoia breeds violence, and it passes down through the ages from our neighbors and our predecessors.

What makes us human is in the center of us in this thing we call the heart. And this heart is about love. It is not about living with guilt and living in fear. Yet, we keep making things more complicated as we "progress."

Is *this* what progress looks like?

"I've caught the sickness of words. I may die talking. It will serve me right."
– Robert Coles, *The Last and First Eskimos*

"My optimism, then, does not rest on the absence of evil, but on a glad belief in the preponderance of good."
– Helen Keller, *Optimism Within*

Misunderstanding and Misinterpretation

Misunderstandings start wars, end marriages, and cause headaches every day. For good or bad, we are born predisposed to unique temperaments and wiring. We are born into different surroundings—and, whether we like it or not, we all have our own sets of strengths, mediocrities, and weaknesses.

It is as it should be; we are all different. So, it's no surprise that interacting with each other while expecting sameness from one another is not only unrealistic; it is disastrous.

Essentially, we're expecting others to see us through our games, self-denials, mediocre social skills, cultural eyes, bungled attempts at communication, and confusing expressions of love and anger. In turn, we expect others to take us as we are, while often, we do not accept them.

And when that does not happen, we end up reaching the wrong conclusions. Hurt, we become intolerant, judgmental, and even violent.

Is the idea that this expectation would work as preposterous as it sounds?

As we broaden our understanding, sometimes we will hear things we don't want to hear. Learning has little to do with comfort and a lot to do with letting new information get through our thick skulls. Sugarcoating destroys more than our teeth and our cell walls. It kills our clarity about life, about who we are, and the justified ways to treat each other.

Seeking new knowledge in accommodating places is not about learning, nor does it work. When I am in a rut or need a different angle, I shouldn't pick up a book or seek a person who supports blind ideas that I am *already* stuck with. That's agreement, not enlightenment. We have zero need to *pretend* we are learning as this **serves** no one, including ourselves, and it only adds to the confusion.

Whom are *you* **serving**?

If one has small ears and a small mouth, they will hear little, learn little, and say little. Please hear us and interact before it's too late.

If one has big ears and a big mouth, they will listen and learn, but sometimes say too much. Please keep things to yourself sometimes.

If one has big ears and a small mouth, they will learn a lot but say little. Staying quiet can be pleasant, but don't let important things go unsaid until it's too late. Interact—step in. Speak up.

If one has small ears and a big mouth, they have little going in and too much coming out. Please hear us, step back, and honor the quiet sometimes.

*People with **small ears can be the most dangerous of all** because they misconstrue much of what they hear, which results in mistaken conclusions and confusion. Confident in what they believe, they create stress and suffering wherever they go.*

Having big ears and a medium-sized mouth would be fantastic.

Which one are you?

If you want to know, don't ask someone who will likely tell you what you want to hear. Ask the person you are afraid to ask. Otherwise, you're just talking to yourself.

"The most important thing in communication
is hearing what is **not** being said."
– Peter F. Drucker

Dumbassery

We all do dumb stuff.

So, it's not about making mistakes, as mistakes are part of learning and life, but rather about how often we make them, what parts of our lives they affect, and how severe they are. Making a poor choice in how we laundered that wool sweater is not the same as making a poor choice in how we pay our mortgage or communicate with family. A shrunken sweater is unlikely to mess up our life, but the latter two examples could and will if this is how we go about things.

Some folks keep making the same, huge mistakes over and again, with no relief in sight. These individuals leave a trail of seemingly never-ending difficulties and hurt, with family, friends, and community.

Interestingly, eulogies rarely speak of the person as they were, everyone seems like a saint once they die. Funeral guests are usually polite and say nothing while at the wake, but sometimes when they get in their cars, they look at each other and say, "Who were they talking about? That's not the Bob *I* knew." But I do understand. We want to show respect and let go.

But, why wait until it gets to the point where there is no return? If people refer to you as a problem or getting through to you is akin to herding cats, perhaps you'd be better off using your gift of stubbornness, focus, and consistency, in another area of life.

In simple terms: Wouldn't it be better to be **consistent in solving problems** rather than *consistently* making problems by doing things the same old way that never worked in the first place?

In even simpler terms: Stop being a turkey. If you were an actual turkey, that would be fabulous. But if you're a human, it's time to drop the act.

Perhaps it's time for all of us to develop new habits.

What kind of a trail are you leaving as you go?

The Simple Approach
(Not to Be Confused with Simplemindedness)

I've never heard people state they need more entangled, stressful lives. However, I *have* heard people say, "I love wisdom and simplicity." But how many people do we know that live wisely and simply?

Consider the jumbled, convoluted ideas of social normalcy we are expecting to adhere to. And it seems they are getting more convoluted by the day.

When we're continuously dissecting ideas, we divert them from their purest and simplest blueprint, and the real meaning gets lost. This is not to suggest that there is no truth in complexity, but rather that things are most authentic in their purest form. As in science, the simplest explanation is usually the correct one.

Part of evolving and growing as a human being is **coming to understand complexities** *but* **choosing to act practically**—*not the other way around.* In that case, you'd be a problematic simpleton (not exactly the person others want in their lives). This complex variation in us is the irony of us – our dichotomy.

Gandhi, Mother Theresa, and others like them, had complex ways of thinking. Still, these individuals understood a simple concept: complicated world politics and greed are bulldozing the quality of people's lives around the globe. The attack on fundamental human rights, like shelter and food, for example, encouraged these remarkable people to embrace simplicity while making a stand against greed, corruption, and violence.

Presently, we are living in a confusing, complicated, and overly sensationalized world. Being publicly horrified about any social issue has become a bizarre trend. There is nothing honest in over-scrutinizing and moralizing every word and deed. It's a somewhat desperate and empty attempt to prove that we care.

Don't allow misleading, petty ideas to get in the way of staying connected to what's happening inside yourself and the world around you. Don't fall into reacting but instead choose to act when truly needed. If overreacting was a philanthropic human trait, we would be living in paradise.

Be genuine. Keep matters simple and clear. This way, the ripples will start their path. The rest will follow.

"Any intelligent fool can make things bigger, more complex and more violent. It takes a touch of genius and a lot of courage to move it in the opposite direction."
– E. F. Schumacher, *Small is Beautiful*

Common sense and balance have no political affiliations; they take no sides.

They stand on their own.
They **cannot be pigeonholed**.

Let's stop pretending and saying that the fighting is about a lack of common sense on the other side.

Problems in society do not get resolved because **all sides waste time**. Too many people focus resources and energy on disproving their opponent instead of honestly looking for what works.

In other words: *Some people are more interested in winning than fixing the problem.*

The truth is: Some people believe that life should always be directed in their own self-serving way, whether it makes *sense* or not. This includes political choices.

Most of us have a family member or a neighbor who makes the point. In my case, a well-to-do relative who believes it makes sense to vote for the candidate who will save them on taxes, even if they otherwise do not approve of the politician. Consider the long-term ramifications of this kind of choice on a massive scale.

Or in the case of a former co-worker of mine, who insisted that voting for someone purely based on matching her own gender, made sense. Consider the long-term ramifications of this kind of choice on a massive scale.

Or an elderly neighbor who hung out in political circles that she didn't approve of, while waiting for a coveted country club membership. Many agreements, silences, and nodding along the way. Consider the long-term ramifications of this kind of choice on a massive scale.

If it's all about *your* feelings, *your* personal comfort, and *your* opinions – in *your* world, common sense and balance don't exist.

The Genuineness of Quality and the Falsehood of Quantity

Everything we crave and fight for—like love, acceptance, safety, truth, connection, sex, passion, desire, nature, melody, affection, laughter, enjoyment of colors, tastes, sounds, and textures—is simple. These things are primitive. They have nothing to do with complicated subjects like computer applications, mathematical formulas, or grammar.

Almost everything else— outside of these simple but powerful cravings— is made up of fillers. When we are happiest or most devastated, the fillers don't matter.

For example, the potential for human knowledge seems endless. It is phenomenal, it is useful, and it has its place, but no matter how knowledgeable one might be, feeling smart will never take the place of feeling loved.

In the end, knowledge, and things that are created from it are not what fills the hole in our soul.

Knowledge creates *stuff, which creates **standards** of living*. It is this *stuff* that creates quantity which turns into *fillers*. There is a sort of **fundamental dishonesty in distraction** and it is these *fillers* that, although can be nice to have, can **distract** us from what truly counts and makes us feel connected and alive.

Quality of life, on the other hand, is the primitive, **simple stuff**. Feeling good about yourself depends on understanding the difference between the two: The *filler stuff (standards of living)*, versus the *simple stuff (quality of life)*. Make a list of the two and see what falls where. Try it.

Once we know the difference, we become lighter and more appreciative of what we have and who we are. We also gain a new understanding of the world, connecting these ideas in ways that were not available to us before.

And in the end, time, (as we know it), is the one absolute, nonnegotiable condition of life *no matter where or how we live.*

Make time for each other. **Don't get hung-up on the *fillers*.** Life goes by quickly. Procure every drop that you can.

"All, everything I understand, I
understand only because I love."
– Leo Tolstoy, *War and Peace*

Political Correctness

Some people in our society believe that avoiding certain words will help eradicate social problems like bigotry, discrimination, and sexual harassment.

In this line of thinking, we can create decency and fairness with appropriate words. But I'm afraid that starting this noble quest by socially banning words is distracting us further from the road we need to take.

The way we speak when out in public does not take away the reality of who we are on the inside and behind closed doors. **Suppression is not eradication.** In fact, suppression usually has the opposite effect—a dangerous recipe for an explosive outcome.

Until we address matters like the *accepted superficiality* in society, the *selfishness in our hearts* and in our homes, and our personal fears; everything else is a *facade of empty, proper remarks.* Fairness and kindness don't come from etiquette and a good vocabulary, they are born from what we feel in our soul.

What's inside is what needs to be addressed.
Without it, everything else is a farce.

"It's discouraging to think how many people are shocked by honesty and how few by deceit."
– Noel Coward, *Blithe Spirit*

15

If you intend to love someone by saying the right things, but you don't follow through on what you said, your **intent** *is to love without responsibility.* And it won't work, even if the love is genuine.

If you are nice, pleasant, and polite, yet, are in the habit of taking advantage— the delivery might be soothing, but your **intent** *is a brick in the foundation of evil.* You might think you've gotten your way, but you are sleepwalking through life. You are missing the satisfaction that genuine connection brings.

If your **sincere intent** is to make people laugh, even a tasteless joke can work. Good comedians do it all the time.

If you **intend to love genuinely** but you do it clumsily, a sincere person will understand. An *insincere person will make a spectacle of it because of their own sickly, emotional needs.*

If you intend to make someone feel small but cover it up with gentle tones and polite words, maybe even a smile, it won't work. Other toxic people might laugh, and even agree, but **genuine people will know who you are,** *regardless of the words* you use.

The power in words is the intent that we give them. *Every single word can be used to love or to hurt others.* As with everything else in life, there are exceptions, but those are a rare anomaly.

Words and tone are the delivery, which can be viewed as important on the surface, but in truth, **context** *and* **intent** *is* **everything,** as they are what's **underneath.**

And what we feel underneath, is what's real.

One of the main issues of this struggle is the confusion of what equality means.

For example, our society is steadily moving from old-world, birthright entitlements, (the son of the king is the rightful future ruler of the land, even if he's a half-wit), to distorted entitlements, (every kid deserves a trophy, even the ones who stood around and did nothing).

Is believing that we all start from scratch the same way or deserve the same thing, equality? If that was so, life would be fair.

The truth is, *biology doesn't care about our social opinions* or about how you and I feel about it. There will always be people greater than, and lesser than, we are, and human babies will always be born to different parents, with different sets of hormones, gifts, and uniquely wired brains.

Being humane is not based on equality; it is based on not being evil. If it was about equality, that would exclusively give us the right to abuse something or someone if we thought them less intelligent, less competent, or less worthy.

We have the equal right to be treated with humanity and justice. We have an equal right to feel safe in each other's presence.

But equality is not sameness.

This is the point.

The oversight of this understanding is *the* **giant of** all **misunderstandings**. And this misinterpretation is further confusing our fight for authentic equality.

Equal Pay for Equal Work

If I am doing the same job as you, with the same skill set, experience, and time invested, but you're systematically making two dollars more per hour, I am not safe in your presence.

Knowing this information between us will have a direct, negative impact on how we perceive and interact with each other. It is unavoidable because it creates a debilitating environment—financially, mentally, and socially. Not only for us but also for others around us.

Debilitation is not safe. Therefore, unequal pay for equal work makes me unsafe in your presence.

To dislike someone because of where they were born is **lying to yourself**.

It is pretending that this person had a choice in the matter.

After all, people can't help where they were born or raised. Eight-year-olds don't pack suitcases and say, "I don't like this culture, I'm out of here." Many have no say in it even as adults.

It would be like resenting a pineapple because it sprouted in South America, or an olive because it grew in Crete. It makes no sense. *Consider the confusion and devastation this kind of thinking has caused the world.*

Always remember that responsibility is *only* possible when people have control over their choices and have access to knowledge about other options.

Is it rational, fair, or kind to look down on those who haven't had the opportunities you've had? Does it make sense to say, "I would have done better if I was in their situation," not having been in their situation?

If you have been brought up in safety, what could you possibly know about the systematic debilitation one feels living day-in and day-out in fear, terrified inside their own home? Or living in a bleak, impoverished neighborhood, where one is scared to step outside the front door.

Having this kind of resentment is being angry at the other guy, who didn't get some wonderful thing you got.

Crazy, right?

Could it be your conscience playing tricks on you?
Guilt is eerily powerful and has devious ways of showing up as anger.

Don't let your biased inner voices work against your natural intelligence and your heart. Sometimes it is logical to be compassionate.

Kirk: "War. We didn't want it, but we've got it."

Spock: "Curious how often you humans manage to obtain that which you do not want."

– *Star Trek*

The Pyramid of False Sense of Entitlement

Throughout history, incompetent bluebloods, tyrants, and spoiled children of wealthy families have oppressed and abused the world, believing the world was built and reserved for them.

Now, the above-mentioned pyramid can be easily accessed by others. For example, within the protection of our free society, every one of us can demand due legal process no matter how frivolous or absurd the claim. *Now*, any of us are entitled to be unaccountable in our choices and actions, legal or otherwise.

Is that what we've been battling for?

When does the grand cycle of pretending that we know something we don't, taking something we don't deserve, and claiming things that aren't ours—end?

Or at least slow down?

Maybe the day we truly understand what honesty with oneself really means.

"You have to do your own growing,
no matter how tall your grandfather was."
– Abraham Lincoln

Have you ever heard stories about people who had near-death experiences that changed them into better people?

Our own mortality, shocking us into self-evaluation and realization of what is important. Your daughter's unacceptable purple hair and the questionable lifestyle of the gay couple next door became insignificant.

All of us need our fears rearranged from time to time.

Sometimes there is no tomorrow.
Rearrange your concerns and priorities today.

Using Money as an Excuse for Bad Behavior

Regardless of how money is acquired, whether through career, inheritance, or the lottery, it is never an excuse to lose one's humanity. I've had my fill of hearing people say, "Well, they have money, why should they care? What did you expect?"

The thing is, money can't buy or sell the soul.
If it could, the wealthiest people would have the best souls.

And although being poor can make one humble and kind, if it generally worked that way, the world would be overrun with kindness, as poverty over-runneth this planet.

I have known plenty of wonderful and equally shady individuals on both ends of the spectrum.

Unfortunately, being spoiled or ruined by wealth is common. However, if you are a jerk because you have stuff, you are probably a jerk without it.

Money does not make you who you are; it exposes who you are.

"I'm opposed to millionaires, but it would be dangerous to offer me the position."
– Mark Twain

The Answer is in Doing

I believe it is vital for people to get involved in threaded discussions because it means that issues will get addressed. However, we must be careful not to put too much energy into talking about a subject, and too little in doing something about it.

Overplaying discussions reminds me of old family and marriage arguments where we just go in circles. It's all just a bunch of words strung together—arguing, apologizing, denying, accusing, and explaining ourselves to death—but nothing changes. It is as though we're stuck in a soap opera and the character who has run away, disappeared, drowned, and been abducted by aliens, somehow miraculously keeps coming back.

Dialogue develops movement, but when do we get to the point in a situation at which you and I stop giving explanations and begin the work?

Don't allow discussions (alone) to trick you into thinking the problem is being addressed. Without the next step of action, it's just talk.

"I am not imposed upon by fine words; I can see what actions mean."
– George Eliot, *The Mill on the Floss*

Our Modern, Enlightened Times

Don't we just love looking back 50 or 300 years ago and shaking our heads at how ignorant and uneducated people used to be?

Now we sign documents to hold us to our word. We aren't still dumb enough to go on a handshake alone. Those old plays were hard to follow, now we have reality shows to enlighten our educated minds.

Love letters? Asking for a date? Who has time for that? You can text them whenever, never return a text, or keep it easy by sending an apology on Facebook. At our own convenience, we will hide our social awkwardness and lack of willingness for a real conversation, behind our laptops. We will no longer be expected to take humble and menial jobs that might question our social media status, our gender, race, or our pride. Instead we will wait, lingering on our couches, for management positions.

Are self-dishonesty, flakiness, laziness, and cowardice, what being "less ignorant" looks like?

Yes, stupidity is **timeless,** but so is **intelligence**. Consider what you can do *differently now*, regardless of our history.

The Dangers of Perception in Regard to Humanity

All of us are blind at different levels.

If we are not careful, we can be quick to use our perception as an excuse for cruddy actions and self-serving conclusions. And, alas, most of us are not careful enough.

Some people say, "There is no *one* universal truth; everybody has their own truth."

Of course, all of us individually have our own experiences. This cannot be argued. However, we must be careful with our own truths. We, as humans, have an unfortunate attachment to using and abusing this idea to sometimes exonerate our own questionable, subjective feelings, observations, and choices. Sometimes we want to remember situations and people as we want to remember them, not as they are.

Hurt and **fear** not only **distort** the **simple truth**, but they also fuel *our views*. This is why *perception* is a tricky monster. Every single one of us has been hurt. Every single one of us is genuinely terrified of something.

Consider our history: It used to be that what we personally thought or felt mattered little. Children were to be seen not heard. Adults were to wear and say what was expected. Authority was *the* authority, on everything. Most of the world worked, thought, and expressed itself collectively in their specific societies. All communities were tribal and a few still are. But now, in our society, the scale is tipping heavily toward the other end of the spectrum. What we personally think and feel is becoming everything. In the fight to be our true selves, our perceptions, in our own minds, are becoming facts.

We were taught to bend the knee to all kings in reverence to their power and their word, and now we are in the practice of bowing to no word and to no one, other than ourselves. We were repressed by endless societal and wealth status boundaries, and now we are in practice of ignoring all boundaries.

But does either work? Does living in an extreme mindset ever work?

Aren't there situations, causes, and ideas that should humble us to our knees even today? Are fragile egos, self-centeredness, and superficial confidence, killing our humility? We had better find a balance, and fast.

Projection

It is difficult, if not impossible, to be a decent human being if people turn their own inadequacies, anger, and angst, onto others. It is a way of treating people poorly.

Should I blame or vent my anger on you because of my own incompetence, delusions, insecurities, and stress? Should I make excuses for those I love when they do the same? Is it helpful to absolve others of responsibility by making inadequate explanations when they are hurtful or out of line?

Everyone has bad days, but that is different than *being* someone's bad day. We all make bad decisions in life, but that's different from making others responsible for our bad decisions.

Imagine if *some* individuals stopped projecting and flinging their internal crud onto others, then consider that the word *some* is a huge number in a world of seven billion people.

Now imagine the ripple effect. It would be a worldwide phenomenon.

Ladies...

If none of these apply to you—wonderful.

Drinking causes all sorts of incidents including humiliation, rape, injury, and death. If you can't handle your alcohol, then don't drink. It really *is* that simple. If it's not simple for you, chances are you have a problem.

Is it honest to tell dirty jokes at work, but be offended by an equally dirty joke told by a male co-worker?

Is it honest to pretend you're interested in a guy so he'll buy you a drink or give you attention, then say he's a creep? Does that possibly make *you* the creep?

Is it honest to say that guys are not brave when it comes to asking girls out, but when they do, and we're not interested, we're snooty or even mocking? It takes courage for them to do so. Be gracious.

Is it genuine to say you are fat because you've gained *three* pounds? There is something unattractive in that kind of thinking.

Is it honest or realistic to be manipulative, gossipy, and mean-spirited but expect others to be genuine? Those things do not make any of us beautiful, intelligent, or good. If we want to be surrounded by sincere and quality people, we must be genuine ourselves.

In the long run, it doesn't pay to be a fake. We are all responsible.

"Women are a strange breed. They paint their lips; Show off their inner-wear; Wear butt-hugging jeans; And then they expect men to first notice their emotions."
– Author Unknown

Gentlemen...

If none of these apply to you—wonderful.

Drinking causes all sorts of incidents including humiliation, rape, injury, and death. If you can't handle your alcohol, then don't drink. It really *is* that simple. If it's not simple for you, chances are you have a problem.

Is it honest to say you hate it when women play head games, but not call when you say you will? That is also a game. No one respects a hypocrite. Be open to sincerity. Be afraid of fabrication unless that's what you want because you're afraid of the real thing.

Is it honest to try to impress with money but say a woman is a gold digger when she is impressed with your money?

Do not trick yourself into believing that being a meathead is the same as being rugged, resilient, or self-assured. Being *confident* is real and good. However, *cockiness* is fake and abrasive. Perceptive people know the difference.

Is it respectful, even to yourself, to speak poorly of girls after you've been with them?

If you're not interested don't play games, it spares no one. Find a nice way to say, "No thank you." An insecure girl might not like it, but a genuine woman will appreciate and respect it.

In the long run, it does not pay to be a coward. We are all responsible.

"Don't be a guy, the world is full of guys, be a man."
– *Say Anything*

Sometimes we find the tackiest and the most inappropriate moment to share what we believe. Can anyone honestly say they have never been guilty of this? And, of course, using the label of "free speech" to threaten or incite fear is altogether something else and a different subject.

However, if you find yourself only supporting free speech when it's in agreement with your beliefs, and you attack those who disagree for exercising their right to do so, it is past time for you to seriously reconsider whether or not you actually support free speech.

If free speech only took place at appropriate events, in agreeable venues, by approved people using approved words; it would not be free speech. It would be a marketing event where no type of product is spared. Shoes, cars, frying pans, and even government platforms. Ever seen political debates?

If free speech is about our personal approval, is it still considered free speech?

"People demand freedom of speech as a compensation for the freedom of thought which they seldom use."
– Soren Kierkegaard

Beware of the overly sensitive types; they sometimes hide ulterior motives and chronic shortcomings behind the appearance of caring and sensitivity.

If everything not perfectly said is offensive, how can one ask honest questions, or give sincere feedback?

If it's that easy to hurt our feelings, is it possible that we have a poor understanding of cause and effect? If arbitrary comments and situations are about *our* feelings, do we leave room for anyone else? Is everything about us?

Have you ever known someone who is hypersensitive about what you say to them but takes no care of what they say to you? Self-centeredness is not about being sensitive. It is emotional tyranny toward others. It is about control, image, and manipulation.

If this commentary agitates you and hurts your feelings, you might be one of those people, though you probably would not recognize it in yourself.

If you want to witness genuine caring and compassion, ask someone who has learned how to forgive those closest to them. *Not just saying it but* **living it**. **The forgiving human heart runs on strength, not hypersensitivity**. Talk to the caregiver sitting through the grueling hours as a hospice volunteer or the kid at school who stepped in to protect a helpless classmate he or she barely knew, at great social and physical risk.

However, if this commentary makes sense to you, pay attention. Learn how to spot the fakes from the real thing. It will save you from a lifetime of drained energy, unnecessary commotion, and hurt.

Exposure

What if I called you on the phone and said, "Hey, did you see the poster downtown of Susie at that party? She was so drunk, it was embarrassing. Did you see it?"

Would you think I was crazy? And what if it was 1987 when I called, when social media was virtually nonexistent and there were few grotesque intrusions of privacy like those we see today?

Yes, times have changed but feeling humiliated and gossiped about still hurts and devastates the same way.

Genuine vulnerability and comfort within our own trusted circles are something we should strive for in our personal lives, it is not something to imitate and expose in a public setting.

Public media is that downtown poster that could do wonders for a new bakery or an upcoming band. But in our personal lives, it is a photo of us in our *intimate* moments with our children, family, and close friends.

You know, those 478 close friends we have.

Please reconsider social media in regard to privacy.

"I never said, I want to be alone, I only said I want to be *let* alone.
There is all the difference."
– Greta Garbo

"It's Working for Me"

Have you ever had a car that made noises you didn't necessarily recognize? It emitted mysterious groans, perhaps had ripped seats, windows that wouldn't open, and several other mysterious problems, but it kept running, as in: working.

And maybe you thought it was okay until you caught a ride with someone who had a decent car. A car ride you enjoyed rather than stressed through.

When it comes to vehicles specifically, if the car gets you to where you need to go it's often good enough. After all, we are talking about a car. An object.

But what about when we apply this principle to people? Can something that is just "running" give us what we need and want?

Could this possibly explain the state of many interactions?

Do you find yourself unexpectedly cutting off relationships with friends, potential mates, your spouse, or family members? Do you keep disappearing on people? Are you not clear why? Do your explanations leave everyone confused, maybe including yourself?

Maybe it is time to consider that you might be a *runner.*

A runaway bride, a bow-out-at-the-last-minute groom, a no-show date, a phone call that never comes in, a disappearing interest or friend, or an I-can't-deal-with-this parent or spouse. Going on an adventure or doing something wonderful and positive with your life is not the same as fleeing from the scene.

Running away smells of panic. Sometimes it is the fear of having something amazing. It is a way of protecting yourself through self-sabotage. Running away is a failure at achieving emotional availability, which must take place if you ever want to be close to another human being.

Geography can't fix your chronic case of unaccountability, intolerance, and fear.

As my friend Panama Jim says, "Wherever you go, there you are."

"I ought to go upright and vital and speak the rude truth in all
ways...
God will not have his work made manifest by cowards."
– Ralph Waldo Emerson

To make a more direct point, if you are feeling like arbitrarily slashing someone or doing something inappropriate with a child, your feelings *are* wrong.

What if a person thinks about killing in cold blood but has not acted on it yet, and keeps his feelings to himself? Do you believe those feelings will have no effect on his life and the lives of the people around him? Is it possible for intensely destructive but hidden feelings, to have no influence on an individual's actions or on the energy they put out?

Don't all hideous acts start with feelings that just *are* until they are committed?

Isn't part of having a *functioning conscience* knowing that it is *not* okay to have certain thoughts and feelings? And isn't thinking and feeling those kinds of things partly what being wrong means?

"A noble heart cannot suspect in others the pettiness and malice that it has never felt."
– Jean Racine

Have you ever noticed that people who are identified as killers are often described by those around them as polite, quiet, or sweet? The "nicest guy around," they said, who turns out to be a con artist or a pedophile, hiding behind impeccable good manners and a permanent smile.

How else would they have convinced us it was okay to get close to them?

I'm not saying that everyone fitting this description is one of those people.
Of course not. But as most of us know, even the sunniest people have bad days, open disagreements, and sometimes put their foot in their mouth.

Being **soft-spoken**, for example, comes from the physical makeup of your vocal cords, family habits, personality, and cultural norms. *It **is not an indication of** your character or your **intentions**.*

Take pause around those who are *always* smiling, appropriate, and nodding in agreement. It is not natural. And it's certainly not what being positive is about. At best, they are a fair-weather friend, a not-to-be trusted co-worker, and a fabrication of a person. At worst, they are dangerous.

Consider the danger you could be putting your children in by not being clear with them about this premise. Being personable is great, but practically speaking all it means is that one is 'good at being able to pull others in.'

Don't be naïve. Be smart. Be safe.

I don't necessarily agree with it, but throughout my life I've been told by others that I'm genuine and honest to a fault. I've also been told that I am different than how I come across to others at first.

I realize not everyone is good at reading others or perhaps I am hard to read.

But I cannot help but wonder: If being *genuine* seems to confuse and disconnect people in our society, does that mean that being **fake** is **accepted** and **understood**?

"People understand me so poorly that they don't even understand
my complaint about them not understanding me."
– Soren Kierkegaard

"It is the harmony of the diverse parts, their symmetry, their happy balance; in a word, it is all that introduces order, all that gives unity, that permits us to see clearly and to comprehend at once both the ensemble and the details."
– Henri Poincare

Men and Women are Different

If you honestly disagree with the above statement, there is not much else to say. But if you are on the fence about it, here are a few lines:

Men are not mothers. Women are not fathers. A mother taking her young son into a public restroom is okay. A father taking his young daughter into a public restroom is not.

Men don't generally stress over getting raped while walking to their cars at night. Women do—literally, all the time.

A man will never understand what it is like to have another human inside his body. Perhaps it's not a mystery why men propagated the idea of penis envy. It sounds like somebody got shortchanged, but that's another subject.

Men usually don't care how much your friend's baby weighed when it was born, what day Jane got married, or what Susie or Bob wore to the wedding, but rather what Susie—or in some cases Bob—would look like if they wore *nothing* to the wedding.

I know there are some exceptional women firefighters out there, but I would be lying if I did not say I'd prefer Bob to carry me down the ladder.

*These are **not double standards**; they are **different standards.** As they only could be, when talking about two things that are different.*

Let's stop wasting time with frivolous accusations of double standards so that genuine issues, (like equal pay for equal work), can get the credibility and attention they need.

The Confusing Fight

The fight for equality between the genders has further confused men and women about each other and about their own roles. We are both protectors and nurturers, but our missions are not the same. Of course, there are exceptions, but we are not talking about those here.

Throughout history, men have believed they should be in charge. The only way that could happen was via force and control. However, being an oppressor is not the same as being a leader. In fact, it is the opposite. When we subdue others, we regress.

Although we are all responsible, the main mission of the male counterpart is to be the protector and the female counterpart is to be the nurturer.

If a person with a knife attacks a couple, will the woman step out in front of the man, while the man shrieks and hides behind her? It doesn't mean the female cannot defend herself or fight, or that there are no exceptions to this scenario, it just means she's not likely to be as good at it as he is since this is his natural genetic makeup.

Even in the Viking days when women fought alongside men, the men still stepped out in front of their wives when intruders showed up at their homesteads. It was their main function to protect. This is what a good protector does best.

And how many stories have we heard of grown men going down in battle, crying out for their mothers or lovers in their last moments between lucidity and the other side. When facing death, we go to the heart. That is where nurturing takes place, and it is what a good nurturer does best.

The male counterpart is the guardian and the female is the emotional interpreter. Men are physically strong, and women are emotionally powerful.

Neither is submissive or dominant. Together they work to create a balance. If one ignores the responsibility, the gift, and the power of the other, a breakdown occurs.

This *is* equality. It is the natural balance. We have the choice to believe whatever we want, but hormones, wiring, and physicality are nature, and nature has its own order.

Competition Gone Wrong

Women and men like to tell each other, "Anything you can do, I can do better."

We joke about it, and humor is great of course, but we also understand that behind the jest, for many this is a real contest. In this case, a contest where there is no winner.

There are better races to be running. The race for cures, for the end-zone, and for a window seat on a road trip. Races should be for human advancement and for fun, not for petty contention. At this point in our social ridiculousness, we might as well be running around yelling, "Winner, winner, chicken dinner," which would probably be more interesting than the present defeatist attitude.

In simple terms: Take care when competing with those close to you.

Competition in close relationships, unless done in a healthy and connected manner, destroys trust, confidence, and friendship.

We need to chill out about this kind of confusing rivalry so that we can have more awesome dinners, laughter, and more great affection.

"Take someone who doesn't keep score,
who's not looking to be richer, or afraid of losing,
who has not the slightest interest even
in his own personality: he's free."
— Rumi

There is an old proverb that claims any gift you are given, if ignored or used to abuse others, becomes a curse. In this case, it is a curse to the abused, the abuser, their family, our society, and **humanity, which is ours too**. Physical strength is a gift of protection and a responsibility to be used for good, not suffering.

Is it possible to be loved by anyone if one is feared by everyone? Being hated by others for the abuse one inflicts does not seem like a thing anyone would want in their life. Yet, the abusers keep at it. Makes one question the reasons behind it, their intelligence or perhaps the possibility of undiagnosed mental illness. Past family abuse comes to mind as well. But somehow the worst reason of all would be something horrible and simple, like being a lousy human.

If you are not a person of faith and an abuser, once you are weak yourself, you will be abused. Who will want to protect you? I would imagine no one.

If you *are* a person of faith, how will you look Him in the eyes and explain why you hurt someone small or someone with less power?

Faith and honor insist on justice and the protection of that which cannot protect itself. This includes humans and animals. Do you think He will punish other abusers, but *you* will be special in His eyes?

It is terribly difficult to wrap a working brain around the concept that being abusive is a way of getting "your way," or is rewarding, (in your conclusion), for today or for your future.

Is being photographed while walking through the airport the same as being photographed by some creep in the bushes while you are in your robe taking the garbage out on a Sunday morning?

Unlike constructive and truthful conversations, which support and direct actions in a population, toxic rumors and gossip destroy communities.

The only interesting question about **gossip** *is why any conscious person would voluntarily want to "know"* **inaccurate, petty,** *and* **mundane** *information.*

Every time a famous person steps outside of their home, the potential attack and shark-like feeding frenzy is always lurking. Every time a local person steps out into a busybody neighborhood, the same kind of shark-like fixation and feeding frenzy takes place but on a smaller scale.

Note: Frantic feedings are part of a shark's natural order.

Which brings me to the question: Are nosy people, who enjoy gossip frenzies a part of the natural order of humans? Or are they naturally lousy people?

P.S. Shark lovers alert! Please don't send me angry emails for comparing your beloved shark to such animals as humans.

Have you ever had someone confide in you, entrust you with something important, spill their guts to you, or ask for advice but then get upset if you disagree with them? Or if you challenge them, they say, "It's none of your business! How dare you?"

Which is about as sane as someone inviting you inside and then yelling, "Hey! What are you doing in here!?!"

If you solicit someone for advice, expect that you will get it.

That's kind of how talking works.

If we don't want any feedback and just want to vent, that's fine, but we have to ask if that's okay first. We can't expect people to sit there like posts and stare off into the distance while we emotionally vomit on them. Give fair warning if you want blind support.

Ask yourself: Am I looking for agreement, or honesty?

All too often people refer to sex as the superficial side of intimacy between two people. It is described as a less authentic part of real love and referred to as somewhat inappropriate and even taboo.

But if that is true, then why does something having to do so little with the authenticity of the love, belong at the top of the list of the undoing of relationships?

People aren't being honest about this.

The truth is that without sex; your partner, no matter how wonderful, is your roommate.

Inevitably, everyone wants it. There are always exceptions but for most people, amazing, intimate sex is the goal. However, few are ever properly taught about sex.

The human race is, for the most part, stuck in uneducated, inept, and mendacious sexual relationships. These leave a wake of unhealthy and unrealistic ideas, toxic family secrets, and hypocritical political and social judgments.

Ignorance is not bliss, especially in this case.

Stop pretending. Stop judging irrationally.

Start talking.

An Overactive Worrywart is a Burden to Others

If someone is having a rough time, the last thing he or she needs is our *excessive* fussing and expressions of worry.

If my intent is to help, then I will help in the way they want me to help, not in the way it makes *me* feel better.

After all, it's about *them*. Right?

Privacy Versus Secrecy

Privacy: You're going through a divorce. You are devastated and not ready to talk about it with your family. You tell them about the divorce but let them know you will fill them in on the details when you are ready.

Secrecy: You pretend things are fine.

Privacy: You and your spouse are having problems and the kids want to know what is going on. You say, "I will tell you what you need to know because it's important that you know what's going on in *our* home but try not to worry about it. We will figure it out."

Secrecy: You pretend nothing is wrong or tell them it's adult business.

(They only live in the house. Leaving them confused and to their own imagination when they are scared, will have no effect on them. They are only kids, they don't understand anyway. Right?)

Privacy: Your cousin gets caught molesting a kid. The whole family is shocked and devastated. They go to the police and turn the cousin in. Some of the family move to where people don't know the relation so they can have normal lives. Some of them stay and do their best to hold their heads up with dignity. It is difficult but they do what must be done.

Secrecy: The whole family is shocked and devastated. They decide it's best to remove any children from his or her presence, but they keep it in the family because it's humiliating. What if he or she loses their job? What will the neighbors say? What will the pastor say? One of the aunts decides it is an atrocity to put other uninformed parents and their children at risk, and she turns the person in. Some of the family members turn on her and treat her as if she is a pot-stirrer and the problem.

Privacy creates safety and trust.

Secrecy breeds paranoia and betrayal.

Acquaintances Versus Friends

Acquaintances are people who you know in passing. You might hang out in the same circles. You talk about the weather, tell them about the great fishing trip you went on, or compliment them on their great taste in shoes.

They are not the people you'd call if you got into a wreck or invite to join a close-knit family dinner. You do those things with close friends.

There are always exceptions but referring to acquaintances as close friends might offend real friends and scare off actual acquaintances.

Keep titles as genuine and clear as you want your relationships to be.

Friends and "Friends"

Real friends are vaults with your privacy. They keep their word. They are not jealous when you are doing well. They are not passive-aggressive when upset with you. They don't give you self-serving advice. They keep you in the loop on things that you need to know. They are open and honest about what's going on in their life. They don't blindly agree when you are clearly wrong because it suits them. They want what is good for you and those you love.

Genuine friends stand up for you and they do not drag your name through the mud if you stop being friends. They do not contribute to a problem you might already be dealing with, and they certainly don't make problems for you.

Friends make things more fun when you are having fun and make life more bearable when it is unbearable.

Life is messy. Shit happens. Who do you want to help you make it out in one piece? You may not be spotless, but you will be presentable. "Friends" would never be able to pull any of this off in the long run.

Be flexible in life but remember it is healthy to know when to go with the flow versus when to make a stand. It's also good to know who is who.

Chance is something that happens by accident, opportunity, and coincidence. Purpose is made of meaning, design, and creation.

It is not clear why the world is so bent on proving that it's one OR the other. **Why can't it be both?** People sometimes laugh when I say this, but people also used to laugh at the idea that the earth wasn't the center of the universe. It was also once believed the ape was a mythical creature and that the world was flat.

The simple truth is, there will always be a time when we do not know what we do not know. Claiming anything else is a conscious fabrication.

Philosophers, writers, and scholars throughout history have warned us not to separate **God** *from* **His elements**. *God being purpose and creation. Elements being opportunity and evolution.*

Life is full of facts, feelings, and intuitions. Intuition has little to do with facts, and facts have nothing to do with intuition, yet they work together. We already know that good, evil, mediocrity, the ripple effect, reasoning, choices, order, and chance—exist.

I don't find it hard to believe that **purpose** *and* **chance** *are* **entwined**. *I find it hard to believe that some people are willing to kill each other just to prove otherwise.*

Focusing on conviction in faith or conviction that God does not exist, is like looking through a microscope. You think you are seeing everything because you can see the tiny cells, but you can't see the building you are sitting in.

Everything is connected. Isn't it plausible that it is **all one**?

How do we know that coming to this understanding is not what makes us *better* humans in the eyes of a Supreme Being and more *evolved* humans in the eyes of science?

Wouldn't the belief that it's *all one,* help resolve two great evils: hate and war, which are a direct cause of conflict over who believes in what?

"Apparently, there is nothing that cannot happen today."
– Mark Twain

One can say, "My marriage wasn't *meant* to work-out but there's a reason I went through it. I sure learned a lot. It all depends on how you choose to perceive it. I choose to be positive and take it as a learning experience."

But what about the little boy with cigarette burns on his arms? What about the innocent who are killed in war, while others watch in horror? Or the little girls kidnapped by human traffickers to be sold into the sex trade?

Is this what is *meant* for them? Is that part of *their* bigger plan? And what exactly are they learning?

Is it always about perception?

I wonder about the hungry woman who witnessed her son and husband slaughtered and her daughter dragged away by dirty men with guns. I wonder what we would feel if we looked at her and said, "Things happen for a reason and this is what's meant for you." Would we be teaching her about being positive?

Maybe it's a poor comparison, but it reminds me of those born with a silver spoon in their mouth, saying, "I don't care about money." While sleeping in soft beds, safe houses, and speaking with lips connected to full bellies.

Perceptions of how we see choices and reasons **are** easier when we have **options**.

If things always happen for a reason, and it's not all good, does it mean it was *meant* to be bad? Was the woman in my circle of acquaintances, (her pet got caught in a fluke accident involving a car and a retractable leash), *meant* to run over her own dog? What larger purpose could that have served?

Do we know what we are saying?

My life is full of stress and ups and downs, and my attitude is of the utmost importance. My perceptions of life carry a lot of weight. On the other hand, I am aware of the reality that I live in the privilege and luxury of a free society—my perceptions being greatly influenced by that freedom.

Is it possible to justify other people's pain through *our* beliefs in a grander plan that satisfy *our* ideas? Can we feel and think this way and still be altruistic?

How did some of us become so complacent with injustice and suffering?

"There are different kinds of spiritual gifts but the same spirit is the source of them all."
– 1st Corinthians 12:4

A Beautiful, Creepy Home

Many years ago, I watched a talk show with several different religious denominations represented. I believe there was a rabbi, a Catholic priest, a pastor, and a couple of scientists. I know it sounds like I'm about to tell a bad joke, but this was a real discussion.

I don't remember many of the details. What I *do* remember, however, was their shocking message. One asked what kind of parents would put candy on the floor, tell their two young children not to touch it, leave the room, then throw the kids out of the house after they eat the candy. Only a complete lunatic would treat his or her children this way. Right?

They were discussing Adam and Eve and their banishment from the Garden of Eden for eating from the tree of knowledge. It was pointed out that the two of them were innocent and unknowing. Essentially, they had the mentality of children. In great irony, it was Charles Darwin who said that humans don't have the intellect to speculate about God. It would be like a dog speculating about Newton.

I am not here to address whether the failure of Adam and Eve happened or not, or what it would mean.

I am here to ask how it applies to us.

What if you saw your neighbors handling their children this way? What would you think of them? What would you do?

Like many people, I struggle with the highly agitating thought about what is at the end of space. And if there is an end—what could possibly be, where there is nothing?

So, for the sake of sleeping, I try not to think about it. Lest it make me crazy. All I can do sometimes is ask questions, and struggle with the fleeting satisfaction that I am unlikely to get a satisfactory answer—and that will have to be enough.

What I *can* answer for myself, with relative certainty, is that I don't have the power, or the ability to understand the idea of God. I can only *hypothesize*. A strong word considering the vast and unreachable subject.

But I do have other questions, which so far in history have produced only additional dubious answers. Is making an everyday mistake the same as being evil? It would have to be. How else can we even consider that we are all born sinners? Many people go through their whole lives being good and taking care of others. They have no cruel bone in their bodies, but they still fall under the same premise.

How does having free will, under someone else's plan, exactly work?

Is an *involved* supreme-being *involved* when He doesn't step in? Is erratic parenting *involved* parenting? What is the agenda of the people attributing this inconsistent quality to the Creator?

Is it suspect that these same people are the ones who tell us that they are full of knowledge about the path to salvation? Are these same individuals horrified by their own mortality? If one claims to have a monopoly on understanding God and the universe, what exactly is that person saying about themselves?

To be clear, I am not looking for an outcry of answers considering you probably don't have them either. Faith is about a personal inner knowing, not about public explanations.

My intention here is not to shed doubt, but simply to say that if more of us accepted or even considered that we don't have the answers, we would be more likely to mind our own glass houses.

This would likely lead to less arguing, alienating, belittling, and killing each other over who knows more about God.

And wouldn't *that* be a miracle?

"I mean, it's no great surprise that savages have no prophets. God didn't really get interested in mankind until those nice white Neolithic farmers came along."
– Daniel Quinn, *Ishmael*

Gay

What if Jesus had taken in a homeless child and the child turned out to be gay? Do you think he would have thrown him back out on the street? Shunned him? Mistreated him? Killed him? Based on his record of hanging out with lepers and prostitutes, I highly doubt it. It would go against everything he taught and represented.

Jesus wasn't a separatist. About the only thing he separated Himself from was the superficial piety of the religious leaders of that time.

Can you really, in the most earnest corners of your heart, believe that *any being* who represents compassion, kindness, and love, would expect you to alienate or abuse your own child? Or be cruel to anyone for being gay?

Do you believe that you have higher standards than Jesus had?

Whom are you emulating?

Rectitude

Do you believe we are saved by righteousness?

Is it possible to be righteous if I believe that *my* opinion and *my* belief system, that serves *my* purposes, *my* path, and *my* conscience, are the only truth? Is it possible to be righteous while basing my entire belief system, for myself, in a way that makes *me* feel good? Is it righteous to say: I know I'm right about God, you are wrong, and you will pay for it.

If righteousness is about a pure heart, goodness, and faith, does it have room for any of this?

Have you ever spent time around someone's family or a new circle of friends and think, *"Dang, these people are oafs."*

They have good jobs and financial success, their children have scholarships, they have decent social skills, and they have seemingly respectable homes. How is it that these outwardly smart people seem miserable and not too bright once you get a closer glimpse? They have weak connections within their own family and only get along on FB and Christmas photos. They have superficial friends and "amazing" children you want to strangle.

What gives?

Consider: Our society places **surface monetary success** *first*, such as image and social popularity, which is what life looks like from the **outside**.

Emotional intelligence, in society, comes *second* or *not at all*. It is the success of what life looks like on the **inside**. It's about knowing how to love, feel connected, and how to get along with each other.

The first is good, but without the second, what's the point?

Mass murderers, tyrants, and bullies throughout history would have been powerless without support from the common herds who advocated for them.

This is why activism, even with good intentions, can be dangerous. Almost everyone wants to belong somewhere. Many people uphold questionable ideas or stand for nothing when standing alone.

Ask yourself: How many individuals do you know that can think for themselves? And how many of those that do, think for themselves *and* do it with a clear head? I've known some lovely folks throughout my life, but very few of them can do so. In fact, I can probably count them on my hands.

Beware of movements. They're made up of people.

"Insanity in individuals is somewhat rare;
in groups it's a rule."
– Friedrich Nietzsche

Mediocrity

Mediocrity can be akin to being too comfortable for your own good. As with bread or marriage, staleness can easily turn into a full plate of a stagnant, barely palpable existence.

Take care. Step out of your box once in a while and ventilate your lackluster life.

Don't let your four walls lead you to a point where you're looking at others with bitterness and scorn. It is always good to remember that a mix of comfort and mediocrity leads to taking things for granted.

And taking things for granted leads to loss.

Being Unique

There are billions of us on this planet, so it is understandable why many people want to see themselves as unique. Yes, we are all different in our own way, but it would take a particularly *different* person to stand out among that many individuals.

The most telltale sign of someone who is not unique is a person who doesn't seem to fully comprehend what distinctiveness means in practical terms.

Those who are genuinely unique sometimes hide it from others because it can mean loneliness. It can mean not fitting in. It can mean being chronically misunderstood. And more often than not, it means being a target.

If you are different but beautiful or creative, people can be jealous and cruel. If you are *just* different, they're just cruel. In such scenarios, being generic can be a sort of a strange gift.

But then again, if you truly stand out above the rest and also happen to be courageous, in your own earthly way you might be able to perform miracles. Keep this in mind at all times. You never know when an opportunity for a miracle might arise.

Always remember: Being generic and being unique can be equally painful, just as blending-in and sticking-out are both a gift and a curse.

Be careful what you wish for. And be kind.

Phrases like 'Be the best that you can be,' and, 'Give a 100% every day,' are good motivators but they can also be problematic. Sometimes expecting others to do their best—no matter what, does not leave much room for mistakes.

Or for being human.

Yes, doing your best and giving a 100% every day can get you what you want, which *can* lead to happiness, but it can also lead to misery.

Some people are wired for competition. They thrive when their limits are pushed. For others, placing that kind of an expectation can have disastrous consequences.

Parents, for example, can wreak havoc on their children's wellbeing by putting unrealistic expectations on them. For those who are predisposed to depression, anxiety, or simply have a 'non-Olympic athlete' approach to life, will not process this type of expectation the same way. Sometimes pushing a naturally competitive kid, even further, can have the direst consequences of all.

We are all different. That is the point. We all want and need different things.

Suggesting that if you don't have the 'be the best you can be' attitude, somehow makes you less-than, or negative; is negative in itself. It can be destructive for an otherwise well-functioning person.

It is good to say: Don't be lazy. Try new things. Don't be a big baby. Move your slow ass. Be on time. Don't cut corners. Wash them dishes. Learn new skills. Give it your best shot and see what happens.

But do not confuse building character with being unyielding. Or expecting your son or daughter to be something they are not.

Teen depression has skyrocketed, and suicide rates have tripled since the 1960's due to a variety of factors (rawhide.org). Among the top on the list are academic and competition pressures. If you are a highly competitive parent and are thinking: *Not my kid—* think again.

Grow up. Be a tough mentor not a controlling tyrant.

Let your kid be a kid and let them grow into *their own adulthood.* You've had your chance to be who you want to be, let them have theirs.

Sometimes a Rake is Just a Rake

I hear people saying that old cartoons are too violent.

"Tom & Jerry used the rake violently." "Elmer Fudd is aggressive and trying to kill Bugs Bunny." "The poor rabbit," she said.

As one of my friends perfectly put it, "If my 10-year-old can't tell the difference between getting hit with a cartoon rake versus a real rake, I suspect we have bigger problems."

I suppose it does appear easier to blame cartoons, when our kids show aggression or mean-spirited behavior, rather than consider our parenting skills. How can we teach our children about what it means to be aggressive and violent if we can't recognize it ourselves?

Parents, please. Let us stick to focusing on resolving real problems. There are plenty of them.

Those Who Can't See Themselves as They are, Fight to Control Others

Have you ever noticed that the same people who often fight for control seem to have no control over themselves? Control over their nerves, anxiousness, temper, passive-aggressive reactions, emotional outbursts, shopping sprees, finances, obsessive thinking, overeating, addictions, and the list goes on. They also tend to be fast to point their finger at others.

It's interesting what motivates us to act as we do.

A *common* example of this hypocritical and crazy-making behavior is a person who habitually buys expensive things he or she cannot afford but will make a huge fuss when other family members buy simple, necessary things. Or individuals who micromanage people around them due to the chaos in their own minds and lives.

An *extreme* example would be Hitler, who wanted to control genetics in his populace and wipe out dark eyes, dark hair, and smaller statures. Apparently, he wanted to wipe himself out but instead turned on others. He wanted to control traits that he hated in himself.

Self-hatred, narcissism, and chronic unawareness are different kinds of diseases. Their first dose of medicine is to take a good, long, painfully honest look in the mirror.

Jealousy Versus Valid Insecurity

Understandable, valid feelings of insecurity are due to something that *has* happened or *is* happening in your life, a conflict in need of resolution. A justifiable insecurity that needs attention and care.

However, pure envy, also known as jealousy, is irrational and different than justifiable feelings of insecurity. Envy is petty and it hides behind the word *love*. It attracts conflict and finds cause when there is none. Jealousy makes healthy people want to run.

Don't let this quintessential, toxic pot-stirrer command your lot and run off the people in your life that are worth trusting.

Learn how to spot the difference between valid insecurity and irrational jealousy. It will save you a lot of unnecessary heartache.

About Yelling

You don't want to go around yelling all the time about everything. That would be ineffective and unnecessary and could be quite embarrassing.

But when you've run out of patience, and the person you're talking to is like a brick wall, yelling might save you from a coronary. Maybe even murder.

It might even get their attention.

So, whether you are doing the deed or getting yelled at, don't fool yourself. Almost everyone deserves to be on one end of it *once in a while*.

Sometimes volume is required.

Spoiled Rotten... as in Moldy Fruit?

I'm always delighted when I hear people say, "Oh, our little one is so adorable. We just spoil'm rotten. Has us wrapped around his little finger."

Oh good. We don't have enough emotionally incompetent, oblivious prima donnas securing the future of our society.

More, please.

Ownership

There is a difference between holding yourself responsible for exacerbating someone's sour behavior and taking responsibility for that person's actions. A contribution of your own stupidity does not make you responsible for the other person's stupid choices.

We are all responsible, but it is important to know what is ours and what is not.

"You know, as logical as you are, it's
quite irrational of you to expect so much
logic from someone as emotional as me."
– M. Brook

"Although the world is full of suffering
it is also full of the overcoming of it."
– Helen Keller

What if you broke your arm and didn't go to the hospital or you refused to wear a cast? Instead, you put on a long-sleeved shirt, took a couple of pills, and said your arm was fine. Would your arm heal right? Would it heal at all?

What makes you think it is any different with an emotional break?

In this particular case, I am not speaking of serious illness, trauma, or death. Those are different kinds of losses. I am talking about pain that comes from hurting each other by making bad choices.

I do not like using the idea of "getting over" because it gives the impression that all pain eventually goes away, no matter how deep it is. When in truth, some pains never leave completely but get better as time passes. Some wounds will always hurt. Some significantly less, while others will eventually disappear.

Time *is* a healer. However, as with everything else in life, we must remember that because all situations are different, so is the pain within them. But that is the beauty of life. We go on. We trudge through the bad days, we show vulnerability to the right persons, and we stick to the steps and the promises so we can have good days. The more we consciously push ourselves to do this, the more good days we can hope there will be. Hope is a strong creature.

That is what healing looks like.

However, *disconnecting* is different. It is covering up the pain and pretending that it's gone. Staying broken but saying, *I'm fine,* while suffering silently. Perhaps suffering loudly and **committing** the **same self-sabotaging deeds** *that brought the pain in the first place.*

It is our own, private warmongering.

Healing can be daunting, but when all is said and done, it is never clear why pretending you are fine, (which causes more loss and can be more painful), would ever be chosen over an honest attempt at healing.

Healing will probably be the hardest thing any of us will ever have to do, but it is worth it. The other options are even more grim in the long run. Push on.

It's like saying to your kid, "Are you sure you don't wanna potty?" while he's mulishly shaking his head right before he pees his pants. But of course, he's three. You are probably a little older and a little wiser.

It is not intelligent to make a stand about something petty. Not to mention a complete waste of time for everyone, including yourself. If you don't have the power to unglue yourself from being a mule, why don't you at least try being stubborn when it can do some good?

Helen Keller never gave up, and she became an unbelievable communicator even though she was deaf and blind. Nelson Mandela managed to become a lawyer and one of the most prominent figures in the history of human rights, even though the odds were greatly stacked against him. Beethoven, who wrote some of the most amazing pieces of music in history, kept on with his work even after he went deaf. I would imagine that was no easy feat. Marie Curie insisted on an education in the field of physics when women lacked opportunities for education and were sneered at for wanting them. She went on to receive a Nobel Prize and paved the path for modern radiation.

These people were not just innovative thinkers; they were immovably stubborn about that which, they felt, had to be moved.

So, stop arguing with Grandma when it's twenty degrees outside and you don't want to wear a coat. Or with your spouse over who is going to take out the garbage. Stop being stubborn when you've been in pain for a while but refuse to have it looked at. Stop refusing help when you need it. *Start doing things differently.*

Do not be the useless, self-sabotaging, and boring kind of stubborn. If you are going to invest yourself, your time, and that kind of powerful energy, use stubbornness to move mountains— even when you're the mountain.

Use it when it counts.

Whether You are Conforming or Rebelling, You Are Letting Others Choose for You

I don't want to wear this because everybody wears it.
I'm not gonna wear something that nobody else is wearing.

Of course I like that song; everyone likes it.
I don't like that song, it's too mainstream.

I won't go to touristy places; everyone goes there.
I will go to touristy places; everyone goes there.

All of us partake in these types of insecurities at times, but if you are consistently applying this kind of mentality in your life, you're not choosing things that match *your* true tastes and desires. You are letting others make the choices for you. It's ironic, isn't it? You are like the other guy you can't stand, but on the opposite side of the same coin.

Eccentricities of those who can honestly think and choose for themselves are not a result of fighting battles to show who they are. It comes naturally to them. If you must work that hard to fit in or to rebel, you are not following your heart, and it's not real. You're putting on a show, just like everyone else.

Find your own true path. Don't fake yourself out.

"I love it when people say, 'Oh, I don't like Google or Amazon because they track where my orders are placed.' And then they come up to the register and pay with one of their five credit cards."
– E. Shae

Using Judgment is Not the Same as Being Irrationally Judgy/Judgmental

Would you drive 60 mph through a crowded parking lot?

Would you allow your kids to jump up and down on the hood of your car?

Would you go to a traditional funeral in a bathing suit?

Those are judgments. Having good judgment is a matter of having decent human interaction skills, showing respect in different ways, and having healthy boundaries. You'd be a knucklehead to do otherwise.

But, if we believe that everyone who drinks is an alcoholic, everyone driving a Mercedes is snooty, every woman wearing a short skirt is an easy lay, every man is a chauvinist pig, everyone who disagrees with our political party is a nitwit, and every foreigner is here to take a piece of our pie, our conclusions would have nothing to do with decent social skills, respect, or good sense.

Judging what we don't understand keeps us from getting along. It brings out anger, awkwardness, and resentment.

Always remember, we are creatures with countless variations. The word *judgment has had a bad and inaccurate rap for long enough.* **Learn the difference between necessary judgment** and **irrational judgment**. **A simple concept that could change the entire world.**

It's okay to start small. Start now. Spread the word.

It is Not Superficial to Want Beauty

I have never heard anyone say, "When I grow up, I want a cruddy house, a spouse that's not much to look at, and a couple of homely kids." Afraid of appearing superficial, a lot of people end up being dishonest about this subject instead.

For example, nature is stunning. Is it superficial to want a beautiful view of an ocean, a mountain, or a flowering cherry tree? **Humans are part of nature.** Why would an attractive face or beautiful eyes be any different?

Yes, every one of us will grow older and there are more meaningful things to think about, but should a thirty-year-old be pegged as *superficial* for wanting a beautiful partner *now*, because one day they will be eighty?

All people want something beautiful in their lives no matter what that something might be. If beauty really didn't matter, people would choose to buy homes with views of the dump because it would be no different than a view of the ocean. Vincent van Gogh would be just another sketch next to your son's stick people on the fridge, and Armani suits would be made of terry cloth, you know, something cozy.

The difference is that something *beautiful to look at* is not more important than goodness, character, or love—not even close. But as with everything, there is a need here for a sense of proportion.

Beauty is no exception.

About Anomalies

Anomalies in everyday life are like phenomena. They are always there but hidden if you're not taking notice of what's going on around you. Overlooking their value or missing them altogether is one of the biggest mistakes in life.

There have been countless people in our lifetime we misjudged, misread, misunderstood, or left out because we were victims of our own polarized thinking. We believed they were just like everyone else, and we were afraid of taking a chance.

There is always the possibility of one exception in every crowd of ten, fifty, a hundred, or just that one, alone. Consider how many amazing opportunities of love, friendship, jobs, connections, and great affection you have missed by passing up or disregarding possible exceptions.

Keep your eyes open—don't be so quick to believe what you think you see.

What if I told you stories about a man who fabricated passports, procured false names, and lied to people's faces, would you think this man was honest?

What if I told you I knew a woman scheming with strangers and friends, behind her husband's back, would you think she was a decent person?

But what if I also filled you in on the back story and the whole picture: The man was smuggling Jews out of Germany during WWII, and the wife was desperately pulling together an intervention for her addict husband.

Every day there are numerous, small-scale schemes for the sake of saving.

Saving our family. Saving our home. Saving our sanity from the scourge of everyday life. Saving ourselves.

Always remember, in life there is intent, which can be good or bad, and in situations there are always exceptions.

Do not be quick to throw someone away because you don't know the details. Do not be quick to judge those trying to survive using unorthodox ways. They are just on the opposite side of the same coin of those using traditional ways and saying the right things but doing it for all the wrong reasons.

Know the full story. Everything is situational.

Everything.

Age

There are endless examples of misconceptions about age as it relates to life. Here are a few:

Some eighteen-year-olds are more mature than some sixty-two-year-olds. Emotional maturity has little to do with age.

Telling fifty-year-olds they are good looking for their age would be like telling eighteen-year-olds they are homely for their age.

Some people gray at twenty-three and some don't gray until they are in their sixties. Some start balding in high school, while others go to their grave with a full head of hair.

Some hit puberty at ten. Others at fifteen. Some reach their full height at thirteen, and some at twenty-three.

We are all built uniquely, we live diversely, so everyone's body ages differently.

Some people are obsessed with sex their entire lives, regardless of age, male or female, while others never are. Everyone's hormones and natural tendencies are different.

There are intelligent and ignorant people of all ages. An ignorant twenty-eight-year-old is likely to be an ignorant sixty-eight-year-old. The predisposition for having a thick head seems to stick.

Stages of life have more to do with our heart's desire (at that particular time) than with age. Some want kids at nineteen, some at forty-five, while others never do.

Sadly, people of all ages fall to all sorts of health conditions, illnesses, and death.

Age has unavoidable effects for each person, but it's often used as a *seemingly* sensible reason to explain away all sort of things.

When really, it's just you.

For every opinion that is valid and correct, there are just as many that are false. Sometimes people believe what they want, regardless of whether it's true or not.

It is not clear why anyone would choose to compound the disagreements by continuing the false rhetoric instead of doing away with it, but that's a whole other book.

Many men and women do not fit the stereotypical mold of how each is presumed to think, look, feel, or live. Both men and women sometimes ignore the truth about a specific situation or person, which further builds bitterness, confusion, and mistrust. One-sided thinking has been the source of ruin for as long as people have roamed the earth.

We are in a vicious cycle, but now we have broader education, travel, exposure to other cultures, access to libraries, blogs, and the internet.

Most of us are literate. Let's not let it go to waste.

Read. Be brave. Ask questions. Look around. Take chances. Make new conclusions.

Change your mind.

The Pull of Attraction

It is understandable to want someone loving and beautiful, but how often have you found yourself strongly attracted to a person for unclear reasons? Other times you might have met someone beautiful and good but felt less of a pull than with the jerk you've been stuck on for two years.

What is that about?

Having an inexplicable pull of attraction *to* someone is not the same as consciously feeling that someone *is* an attractive, quality person to us. It sounds the same, but it is not. We are not always pulled toward what we naturally love or need, but toward what we have been conditioned to react to. In other words, we are pulled toward what we are used to. In some instances, toward doing the opposite of what we are used to, while trying to escape our past. Either way, we are not following our natural wants and desires.

All of us are made of two things: the natural tendencies we were born with and the things we learn along the way. The traits we were born with are basic, inherent dispositions, needs, and tastes. The things we learned were "implanted" into us by our family, friends, and culture. Some of them fit our nature, while others were corrosive and confusing to our natural temperament and needs.

For example, you might have loved a certain kind of music or hobby because that's how you grew up. Or, you could trick yourself into believing that you're attracted to a person's looks, or maybe because they play soccer, or because they love volunteering. Years later you may realize you have tastes and curiosities that are completely different from people who influenced your life.

If you had an overbearing parent, you can be easily, and subconsciously, attracted to an overbearing partner. If your father was an alcoholic, you might be attracted to others with addictions. If your mother was manipulative, you might be attracted to mates who play you like a violin. It is very tricky.

The person you settle down with, in the long run, is the most important choice you will make because it will have a profound effect on your life.

The next time you feel that pull, ask yourself: Is that what I really want? Or is that what I've been taught to want?

It's never too late.

A Person's Number

There are many variations on this subject. Here is one example.

When we ask about someone, the reply we usually get is something like this: "She is 5'7", has brown hair, is about 140 lbs., 32 years old, has a four-year degree in science. Works for that chemical company I was telling you about. Last year she made over $60k. She lives near the city park, on 16th I think."

That's a lot of digits, and very little (if any) relevant information regarding the actual person. Whether the question was posed for a job or a romantic interest, their zip code and height have little or no relevance on whether this individual is worthy of your time. The right person for any facet of life cannot be boxed into a bunch of numbers describing them. Things like competence, social skills, willingness to listen, attitude, their ability to deal with stress, or any other incredibly important traits, are completely left out in the 'number' equation.

Yet, this is how most people find their jobs, and even mates. Consider how much credibility resumes hold or how online dating sites are organized.

Might this explain why many marry poorly and have jobs they suck at?

We need to re-examine how we go about deciding on what makes a person the right fit for *anything.*

Packaging

We have preconceived ideas of what our ideal match would look like and what kind of jobs and hobbies this person would have. For example, I overheard a rancher say "a cowgirl" when asked what type of woman he was looking for. The thing is, anyone can be good at riding a horse or look good in a pair of jeans. What does that have to do with the powerful needs of your heart and soul? It may sound corny, but it's true.

We look for the wrong things until it's past the wedding date, past the rodeo, past a couple of kids, and one day we look at our spouse and think, "Who *is* that?"

Not too long ago, I heard a woman say she married her ex because he would make a great father, and at first it seemed things were going to be fine. But keep in mind that everything is shiny when it's new. As time went on, the two of them realized the only true connection they had was their kids. Not too long after, they split up. If you're settling down with a man because he would make a great father, then a father is what you'll end up with. What about a husband, a lover, and a partner in crime?

A family friend at fifty-four married a beautiful woman of thirty-one. Everyone asked, "What is this attractive young lady doing with this old guy?" My cousin said they got along beautifully but, of course, most people ignored that part. I guess their compatibility was not as important to others as their looks and their age. Six years later *she* had a stroke and became partially paralyzed on one side. He is healthy and takes care of *her*. I hear they are still like two peas in a pod.

Life is funny that way—it throws curve balls. Societal expectations come and go, but a powerful connection remains. When people fit from the inside, other factors make little difference unless we allow others to poison what we have because of our own insecurities and fear.

If income or age were big factors in having lasting chemistry and getting along, most people would still be happily married, since a majority of the populace in our culture marry within their age group and economic class.

Most couples get together based on those prepackaged ideas. We can refer to statistics endlessly, but the proof is in the pudding. Look around, what do you see?

Nobody wants to wake up one morning and realize that their true attachment is not to the person they live with, but to the person's numbers, image, and stuff.

"Whatever souls are made of, his and mine are the same."
– Emily Bronte

The Fallacy of Being "Ready"

Every day someone out there lets an amazing match pass by because they are scared, or because they are not ready to be with someone.

When people say **timing is everything**, we might think they mean in terms of time suiting our readiness—but we are missing the point. It could be **the moment in time** when the right person walks in, the same person we might never see again.

This is how numerous people end up with the *wrong person* at the *right time.*

The Hypothesis of Being a Big Baby

Have you noticed that when someone we trust tells us something sensible and important that we don't want to hear, we often focus on being hurt by them rather than on the information they gave us?

No one likes to have their feelings hurt, but wouldn't you prefer to know something about your own life than walk around with your head in the sand? And if you *already know*, think of it this way, all they're doing is agreeing with you. What they are saying is, "No, you're not crazy. You really need to do something about that."

If we stepped in for each other more at the beginning of problems, large scale interventions might not be needed as often as they are.

Self-serving family members and friends tend to keep their genuine thoughts from us when we need to hear them the most. They don't want to put themselves out on the line. However, even kind and selfless people will sometimes do this because they fear our reaction.

You have probably heard the aphorisms, "It takes a village to raise a child," and, "No man is an island." They come from the basic idea that it takes family and friends to maintain a growing adult. Puberty does not end growth. Whether we like it or not, everything we do is a group effort because everything has a domino effect. Independence is good but as long as we are around others, there is no autonomous, unobstructed, self-ruling thing called *alone.* That little thing you do will affect others in some shape or form. Especially those close to you.

We all need each other. Don't be childish. Be thankful you have people willing to step in and straighten you out.

If you're thinking *I don't need anyone telling me what's up,* all I can say is be careful what you wish for.

Fighting Well

Knowing how to argue well is grossly understated in our culture. Otherwise, our anger and annoyance will turn into silent treatments—slamming doors, leaving the room, hanging up, screaming—and growing apart. Too often, no argument means no resolution.

That lump we've created underneath the rug, you know, the rug under which we swept our problems, eventually got so big that we started tripping over it. As time moves forward, we walk around the rug and pretend it's not there. Maybe one day we begin avoiding the room altogether. Maybe we go to someone else's room. This is how hurt and loss are made.

Learn how to argue. Talk to someone who knows how to. Get a book. Do whatever. Just learn how to do it.

It will save us from a lifetime of hiding, fighting below the belt, and leaving.

"Father sighed. Please spare me
these arguments of yours."

"Well, whose arguments should I use?"
– Franny Billingsley, *Chime*

Saying Sorry is a Stance of Strength

If you will gladly admit that you are too stubborn, tough, or prideful to say you are sorry, what people in your life are probably *not* telling you is that you're choosing the spineless way out.

When we have truly hurt someone, eating humble pie takes courage. When we've disappointed someone, looking them in the face takes courage. Saying sorry, especially when it is gut-wrenching and humiliating because it is over something important, is damn hard.

Apologizing is not for the weak.

Be courageous. Make amends.

Love is not for cowards.

"First I must say, I have been the
most unmitigated, incomprehensible ass."
– *Pride and Prejudice*

Blame Versus Responsibility

Blame is weak. It is an action that says, "It's all you, not me." It says it a thousand times in many unrecognizable ways and when you least expect it.

Sometimes, it shows up as an argument in which you think you are fighting over who misplaced the keys. Other times blame shows up as a passive-aggressive comment, or an unresolved argument from two weeks ago, or twenty years ago. **Blame** is about **resentment, secrets,** and **self-dishonesty**. The rot of tooth decay and rust cannot hold a candle to this destructive monstrosity.

However: Responsibility is strength. Sometimes it gets angry. Sometimes it fights. But ultimately, when all is said and done, responsibility lets things go. It says, "I'm sorry. What can I do differently?" And then proceeds to do it.

Blame does nothing useful but stir the pot.

It is for you to decide whether you want *blame*, which will compound the situation, or *responsibility*, which will defuse and possibly mend it.

It's your call.

Love is Forgiveness

To love is to forgive. To be clear, we are not talking about horrific acts here. We are talking about the day in and day out, the long and short of it, sometimes stale, overstretched, overtired, stressed, misunderstood, and messy everyday life. No one is exempt from misjudgment, accidents, and folly.

Don't compete with loved ones or keep a scorecard. Acknowledge when they apologize or succeed. Don't hang onto trivial things or bring up old arguments without cause. Let the past be the past and only bring up an old argument if it will help clear things up in the present. Don't say you're sorry but act as if you're not or expect forgiveness when you won't give it. Be reasonable. Act with humility when you've messed up.

Don't be too proud to be happy.

The simple truth of the matter is that *a life that works gives what it wants*.

If we want fairness, we must *treat each other fairly*. If we want clarity, *we must be clear*. If we want forgiveness, we must *learn how to forgive*.

How can life work any other way?

Just because someone has not shown favorable results in his or her life or perhaps is a complete screwup, it does not mean they have nothing good to say.

Some of the cruddiest parents have amazing insights because they see what they could have done differently. Just as some of the world's best mechanics have the shoddiest cars, and doctors can make the worse patients. Sometimes we learn by watching others screw up. We are always teaching each other even when we are not aware of it.

Don't fool yourself. Everyone has at least one subject they can school you in.

Pay attention. Sometimes the advice and wisdom you need comes from the least expected source.

Denial

When we are experts at denying truths in our lives and we make choices based on these denials, there is no stopping the negative chain of events that will follow those decisions, no matter how picture perfect our lies have made us.

It takes courage to see, to acknowledge, and to break old hurtful family patterns hidden behind fear and denial. It takes guts to lead others and ourselves.

The thing is, when we acknowledge the truth, we will also see that we'll have to do something about it. And sometimes, we don't want to bother to open up that can of worms.

Maybe denial seems painless at the start, but in reality, it makes life exceedingly more difficult and often devastating at the finish.

Naivete as an Artform

Naive is:

Believing that our new son-in-law is a good guy because he is polite, has a good job, and dresses appropriately.

Believing our teen daughter is not having sex because she is polite, has good grades, and dresses appropriately.

Some parents believe that if they talk about sex in a secretive, don't-mention-the- weird-cousin-in-the-closet way, their kids are not going to open the door and look.

Believing that *every person* can be good if we give him or her the chance.

Believing that our loving, trim, significant other will still want to rip our clothes off, even if we let ourselves go. Many people have ruined their relationships due to this kind of thinking. Love and attraction are related, but they are not the same.

Believing someone who repeatedly cheats throughout a dating relationship will become loyal once they are married.

Believing that having class is about having money.

Believing that saying something unwarranted but using a polite tone and appropriate words, somehow makes it okay.

Believing that we know what is going on because we listen to gossip.

Believing that a politician is telling the truth because they agree with us and belong to the same political party. This one always gives me a good laugh. Except that none of this is funny. The people who believe these types of ideas also drive, vote, reproduce, and make many other decisions that will, in some shape or form, make an impact on every single one of us.

"Politics is supposed to be the second oldest profession. I have come to realize, that it bears a very close resemblance to the first."
– Ronald Reagan

Referring to a tasteful magazine cover of a beautiful model as *porn* is no different from telling our kids that porn will teach them how to please a woman or a man. As both of these ideas show a dangerously poor sense of proportion, *they also show a gross lack of understanding of context and balance in life.*

One must be clear about the subject of sexuality to raise a socially and emotionally healthy child. If a teenager is not taught the simple difference between a beautiful photograph and a truly disturbing photo, he or she will be confused about women, men, sexuality, and life in general.

Not being *clear,* gives an impression of not grasping what is out there. A healthy adult knows the difference.

Every single one of us needs more education and a good sense of balance in some area of life. This subject is a big one.

Big subjects make for big screwups if they are not clarified.

People sometimes ask me how I managed to raise genuine kids in today's world.

The simple answer is that I did not give them flim-flam and poppycock. I was open about my faults and mistakes, and I didn't allow gross displays of unhealthy competition and selfishness between them. Sugarcoating or hiding any of these monumental issues would have been flim-flam'ing them. Roughly termed: No BS.

When they were little, they did not always understand the words, but they understood the feeling. They eventually understood the idea.

Parents tend to demand excellent grades and good manners, but many allow less than decent human skills. Many parents want their kids to win, which is fine, but winning means little behind closed doors.

You're filling them with excuses when you say, "You're the oldest, so you get to do this. You're the youngest, so you get to whine. You're the middle child, so you get to seek constant attention. You're four, so you get to throw yourself on the floor at the grocery store. You're thirteen, so you get to be disrespectful. You're hormonal, so you get to be mean." This encourages toxic competition within the family unit.

On the radio last week, a child expert said, "We need to be supportive." I agreed until I heard her version of support. She said, "If your toddler throws a tantrum and throws a sippy cup at your head, you should say: *That's not okay, but I love you and I am here for you.*" I laughed for a good ten minutes. Is it possible that she was a comic testing her material?

My kids are still kids. They are a pain in the neck and sometimes I want to throttle them, but they are quite wonderful.

If we as parents are disconnected, how can we teach our children to be connected? Without this crucial association, we will raise a baffled, self-centered crybaby who knows how to put on a convincing show.

How far are we willing to confuse our children by not facing our own inadequacies?

Harmless Fantasy

Santa Clause is real. He uses the chimney as a door, flies around with reindeer, and has thousands of little elves that make toys.

Bunnies lay eggs.
The tooth-fairy gives you money.
Mommy and Daddy make babies by kissing.
Babies come from hospitals and mommy's belly button.

We tell our kids many seemingly harmless things, and when they are seven, or ten, perhaps we tell them the truth. Perhaps we don't say anything, and they learn from other sources. Possibly unreliable sources, like their friends and internet gossip.

Sometimes, we understandably want to soften the blow. However, telling our children some truth or simply saying, "I will tell you a bit now and more as time goes," is better than saying nothing or making up tales. Tales and stories like, "She's a friend of your father's," or, "Kathy went to visit Aunt Martha for a few months." Then six months later cousin Kathy shows up with a baby, and dad is marrying his "friend." Enters: More confusion, more secrets, more awkward exchanges, more uncertainty, and the downfall of trust keeps gaining momentum.

How does one go back as a parent on all these and still sound like a grounded and trustworthy person? We demand their respect but we don't respect their right to appropriate and truthful information. Then we wonder why our kids start questioning the things we say and looking at us with suspicion and resentment.

Is it perhaps because from the time they could speak we have been making stuff up, avoiding necessary conversations, and treating them like they are too inept to learn and understand?

There is more lying around the world about abstinence than just about anything else in existence. And we all know it, regardless of what we say.

In our culture, as recent as 150 years ago people married in their teens or early twenties and commonly died when they were in their forties and fifties. Many were illiterate, few traveled, and most lived in small communities. The difference between now and then is staggering. The irony is that most teens and young adults of that time *were* having sex, but it was within the code of marriage.

I'm not here to say what's right. I am simply stating that expectations and norms have changed—while our physical bodies are the same. People say, "Don't get married at sixteen but don't have sex at sixteen." In this scenario sexuality is being completely taken out of the picture. While society rages, hormones rage. Behind closed doors many homes are wrecks, further contributing to a teenager's already present confusion on how to handle themselves.

If people back then were not getting married so young, would most of them have stayed celibate for another decade or two? That's hard to believe.

One-third of all pregnancies, during early twentieth-century England, (grandparents to many of us), were conceived outside of wedlock (historyandpolicy.org.). It was the ultimate taboo of that time. I realize numbers don't change the morality of the heart, but morality and ethics are rooted in self-responsibility. Irresponsibility makes sex dangerous.

Teaching abstinence, while leaving out the truth about the history of sex in our society, is immoral because it is irresponsible. Being informed about what pregnancy and sexually transmitted diseases do to your body, your family, your pocketbook, your social life, and your heart, *is* a moral responsibility.

For the most part, teaching abstinence doesn't work. Check out research sites, including some Christian-based sites. Better yet, look around your community. Most parents preach to their teenagers to stay away from sex, while many kids don't. Why not encourage teens to wait until they are at least out of high school? They might listen to that because it's considerably more realistic than teaching abstinence. In high school, the gossip and skin-crawling awkwardness around the subject of sex was a serious deterrent for me.

Stop telling them it's immoral. Their ears clamp up and teens are the queens of arguing. Show them the ugliness of what can, and often does happen. Here are a few examples and a good way to use the internet for educational purposes.

Breastfeeding can make your nipples bleed and crust over. It will make your bouncy young breasts turn into prunes. Show them photos of gonorrhea (bacterial infection of throat, genital, and anus) which is most common with people between the ages of fifteen and twenty-four. Tell your daughter what boys *really* say, behind their back afterward. Don't skirt it. Give them specifics. In the real world, showing the unsightly details of rash sex can only help. No pun intended.

Do you believe that talking obsessively about your weight will not leave a convoluted message with whoever is listening, young people in particular?

Do you believe encouraging good eating habits and an active lifestyle are the same as obsessing over a scale?

Do you believe that having a perfect body is what gives you a good body image?

If it were, beautiful people would have amazing self-esteem, but we know that's not true. In my experience, it is often the opposite.

We can choose to blame the media, but who is doing the real damage?

Do what you can to change your mentality about this subject. Stop *over-evaluating* your body. Stop *over-evaluating* other people's bodies.

By judging obsessively, we create turmoil in our own body and mind. It is a good way to make ourselves and others around us miserable, no matter how we look.

That isn't the goal, is it?

Let's focus on action for the betterment of everyday life instead. It will change our conversations and build self-esteem for us and our daughters in the process.

Our world is in crisis.

Wars, famine, sex-trafficking, child porn, abuse, unemployment, healthcare, homelessness, school shootings, drunk driving, inflation, and the list goes on. Meanwhile, some people in power are championing the evils of airbrushing in fashion ads with their valuable time, due to the outrage toward these ads by parents across the country.

We don't like to admit it, but most of us already know that disconnected parents have been blaming song lyrics, drugs, the neighbors' kids, and all sorts of outside factors, for as long as there have been parents and kids.

Sometimes it *is* the neighbor's kids. Sometimes the ads *do* play a role. But there are millions of functioning teenagers who see the exact same endorsements and are not bulimic, anorexic, depressed, or violent. They don't owe $15,000 due to frivolous shopping sprees, and they don't rack up $500 telephone bills for their parents.

Should we change the Constitution to cater to individuals with addictive personalities who can't think for themselves?

That sounds dangerous.

If TV and magazines generally have more influence on my kids than I do, what exactly is that saying? I am the one who raised them. I am the one who talks to them, holds them, and hugs them. I nurse them back to health when they are sick and pick them up from school. I bake them cakes, I hold their hands when crossing the street. I scold them, teach them right from wrong, set them straight when they are off, teach them their self-worth, and show them every day how valuable, smart, and lovable they are.

But the random magazines—created and sold for money by a bunch of strangers—have more influence over them than I do?

It sounds like there is more to this story. At this point I would be asking myself, what is going on in my head and in my home?

> "It's usually an inside job."
> – Sandy Fawcett

It's not clear why anyone would want to be beautiful by looking like someone else.

There are just as many tall, thin, short, stocky, petite, hefty, dark-haired, blond, arched-eye-browed, small-footed, high-cheek boned, straight-nosed, full-lipped, straight-smiled, homely people – as there are beautiful ones.

Not only is beauty in the eye of the beholder, but if it consisted of a specific height, weight, frame, color, or feature, all the beautiful people on the planet would look like the same person. Think about it.

Weird but true.

I don't see any resemblance between Naomi Campbell, Ziyi Zhang, Rita Hayworth, Michelle Rodriguez, or Blake Lively. And I don't see much likeness between Johnny Depp, Paul Newman, Timothee Chalamet, and Sidney Poitier.

If you have a good face it's not *because* you have high cheekbones or blue eyes, but simply because what you have works well together as a unit.

Like everything else in life, when things click, they just do.

Stop picking yourself and others apart over wanting something that doesn't even make sense.

It sounds trite, but it's true: *You* need to do what *you* need to do, to look and feel *your* best.

No need for clones.

"Hey my brother can I borrow
some of your Hey Soul Classics?
"No, my brother, you have to go get your own."
– *Say Anything*

New Consumer Confusion: Missing the Point on an Organic Level

I had a conversation with my eighty-one-year-old mother about the prices of organic food and some of the people who buy it.

Mama: "What do they mean 'organic'?"

Me: "Oh, it just means they are grown naturally."

Mama: "Oh, you mean the way we did back home, and we were too poor to spray them?"

Me (laughing): "Yeah."

Mama: "Hmm, it's good to eat healthy. Very good. But some of them sure sound self-important about it, as if they're enlightened because they're now eating the same way people have always been eating, or because they can afford expensive bananas."

Me: "Yup."

Mama: "Day in, day out. No Safeway if the crop failed. Sometimes we went hungry. We didn't have a flushing toilet either, maybe I should put on airs."

Sometimes it takes a while for it to sink in, but my mom somehow manages to set me straight about *goings-on* even when she is not aware of what's going on.

Is the Customer Always Right?

We have all witnessed it. Some genius who has no power in his own life, or over himself, goes to the restaurant and is rude to the friendly and helpful waitress, or yells at the bank-teller because he overdrew his own account.

People will say, "What a jerk."

Unfortunately, many of these yahoos *like* being jerks. In their warped minds it means they are the ones with power in the situation.

When people are narcissistic and small inside, they will grab "power" anywhere they can find it. It's similar to those who abuse children, pets, spouses, or anyone that cannot defend themselves. The aggression inside them is always searching for this sort of a depraved acknowledgment.

In other words, calling them 'jerks' will often encourage them.

This is an important distinction. When you see it, call it for what it is—weak. This might actually discourage them; nobody wants to be seen as weak.

Is the customer, always right? This mantra invites lousy behavior from some. Maybe the two common signs we see at establishments should be combined and read:

"We strive for great customer service, but we have the right to refuse service to anyone."

Spread the word.

Research, Lawsuits, and Captain Obvious

According to an array of research articles in magazines and on the internet, religious people live longer. But did we need years of examination and countless pages of data to tell us that if you lead a clean, spiritual lifestyle, you will likely be healthier and live a longer life? I don't know, maybe these guys doing the research were trying to use up grants and make careers for themselves.

People started paying attention to nicotine addiction after research showed that smoking kills. It became a debate. Really? Ever seen the soot from smoke on campfire rocks? Do we need an investigation to tell us that if we smoke like a chimney, we'll *be* like a chimney?

I keep seeing random articles and hearing people say that teens with an "online life" are more likely to start drinking, smoking, and having other problems. Hard to believe that an individual with a penchant for unhealthy, addictive behavior online is likely to have healthy interactions in person.

Research says 43 percent of teen males say they were coerced into unwanted sex by mostly female acquaintances (apa.org). That means that four out of ten teenage boys had to be talked, or forced, into having sex. Hmm.

We know that research has its place, but we must be careful with studies and statistics because some have their own agendas— and not always good ones.

Big companies want us to believe their research so that we will buy their products. Certain social leaders want us to believe their rhetoric, so we'll be scared and do as they say. Politically correct soldiers want us to believe their research so they can micromanage us. Some people push for a masculine society, a white society, some for a feminine society; it's endless and it comes in all forms.

Many individuals and groups are long on having an angle, but short on honesty.

Where does self-accountability come in?

Research gives us information; it does not take our responsibility and power away from making our own intelligent conclusions and decisions.

With some knowledge the only requirement is that we are not in a coma.

Wake up. We are all responsible.

Laptop Courage

Many become "brave" while sitting at their computer and posting comments on the internet.

Here are a few examples:

People referring to an eighteen-year-old, dating a seventeen-year-old, as a pedophile. But it's two high-school seniors attending the same class. And what would that say about some of our grandfathers who commonly (as men in their 20s, 30s, and older) married our grandmothers when they were sixteen?

People calling Jimmy Carter an "imbecile" because of his book, *A Call to Action*. Regardless of what you thought of his presidency, it is a courageous book that addresses violence toward little girls and women around the world.

People trashing each other and outing secrets about their family and friends.

People degrading and threatening musicians and their families because they hate the culture the song came from.

This is frightening. What is happening to our more literate, advanced world?

Writing uncultivated commentaries reminds me of people running their mouths when they are liquored up, saying things they wouldn't say sober.

In this case, people are saying things they would be too ashamed to say in person.

Please. Stop.

The Grey Area of Guns

Generally, when the subject of guns comes up, there's either someone yelling "Guns are my life!" Or, "Guns are evil!" And they are both foaming at the mouth. Kind of hard to address the issue or meet in the middle when you have those two on opposing ends.

For example, if you live in the boonies or work in the woods, you would be foolish not to own a gun. If you have not experienced the lifestyle, I suppose it is difficult to understand the need.

However, the obsession many have with guns is insane. Just about anyone can get their hands on all sorts of powerful guns, including ones you would not use for hunting, or as a concealed weapon for self-protection purposes.

I mean, what could go wrong? Right?

There are a lot of unstable people out there. The everyday, seemingly normal cretins are the bigger problem since they are harder to discern from the truly disturbed, making it more difficult knowing whom to watch out for.

In the old days, people ate and lived off the gun. Most of them had *one* rifle. There was no local Albertsons, yet they didn't have an arsenal. They also had more respect for the gun.

But some who are against guns will disagree with me. And some who are for guns will disagree with me. Not sure about what, but they will find something.

While the truth of the matter is, until the masses and our governing bodies address the paranoia and corruption that exists on both sides of the debate, I am afraid we're kind of screwed.

If you're paranoid, you're not thinking straight. If you're corrupt, you don't care if you're not thinking straight. Other things are controlling your mind.

Are you, without realizing it, helping either side get more and more out of whack? And if you could, what would you do to defuse this monstrous problem?

"It's hard to talk to a man when his head is up an elk's ass."
– M. Sherman

Drones have killed droves of innocent people, including children.

Can something dirty birth a clean slate for future freedoms?

Will it bring trusting allies?

It is hard to imagine someone saying, "We killed sixteen civilians, seven of them children, but outside of that we've made some really good headway."

I understand that interventions are complex, but I will go out on a limb and say that true progress and the deaths of the innocent are *still* mutually exclusive.

"If all prayers were answered there would be no law in nature, it would be chaos. It would make things going on now, seem normal."
– S. Rhys

Hypocrisy

Parents are hypocritical with their kids.
Kids are hypocritical with their friends.
Companies are hypocritical with their employees.
Governments are hypocritical with their people.
Countries are hypocritical with each other.

Hypocrisy is one of the few human traits that can single-handedly
and at the speed of snapping our fingers; replace loyalty, morale,
and trust—with resentment, hatred, violence, and retaliation.

If you want a good family, community, country, or world, we
cannot let this tricky, ego-feeding vermin go unaddressed.

So, start addressing.

Every single one of us has our hands in it at some level.

"Before you embark on a journey
of revenge, dig two graves."
– Confucius

The Appearance of Having Options

Ever been stuck at a grocery store aisle because there are so many choices that it puts you in a visual coma?

Buying toiletries, cereal, or socks these days can be quite confusing, time consuming, and even stressful.

Choices are nice, great, in fact. But do we really need a hundred different types of hair conditioners or two dozen dish soaps to choose from?

Does it make us feel like we have freedom to choose because we are choosing between a hundred different types of shampoos?

We live in one of the most powerful nations in the world. Our cultural, political, and socio-economic landscape is like no other. If one tried to bottle-neck what would genuinely represent us as a people, it would be hard, if not impossible to do.

Yet, we have *two main political parties* to represent us, manage us, and oversee our 328 million citizens, and 3.79 million square miles of land.

Which begs the question: Do we have power in *important* choices, or do we have the illusion of choice—via shopping?

A man is beaten and arrested after police officers believe he is displaying threatening gestures (libertycrier.com). As it turns out the man was deaf and was trying to communicate using sign language. Once the peace officers realized this, they tried charging him with resisting arrest. Were these officers, zombies? It's a fair question.

A twelve-year-old girl gets arrested for doodling, "Lex was here 2/1/10" on her school desk (huffingtonpost.com).

Federal agents raided an Amish farm at 5 a.m. because they were selling unauthorized milk (businessinsider.com).

A fisherman receives a $500 fine for untangling a whale caught in his net. In court, he was told he should have called wildlife experts instead (capecodtimes.com). What if the whale suffocated while waiting for them? Imagine the outrage if he had done nothing.

A husband faces five years in prison for reading his wife's e-mail (abcnews.go.com).

A ten-year-old girl brought a steak and a set of utensils to school for lunch. She was arrested for using the small steak knife (caffertyfile.blogs.cnn.com). The school defended itself saying they were following safety protocols. The girl faced a felony charge with no concession from the school. Forks are weapons too, should we ban them as well?

Can you imagine the trauma these arrests caused? Consider the long-term effects of how these experiences will linger with these people for the rest of their lives. This is how paranoia can be born. Will these folks trust our governing bodies? How will they feel when they see a cop car drive by? Will they be comfortable going to their school administration in time of need?

I feel outraged. If you are not horrified by these examples, you're not connecting the dots here.

These types of situations could happen to anyone, including you or one of your kids.

Rules should never overrule common sense.

Be outraged. Stand up for each other. That's often the first step in making things right.

In Brooklyn, New York, in 1989, a man was wrongfully convicted of murder. He was released from prison after twenty-five years when a team of attorneys led by Kenneth P. Thompson turned up new evidence clearing him of the conviction (nytimes.com).

In Holdenville, Oklahoma, in 1970, a man was wrongfully convicted of murder (usobserver.com). He was released from prison after serving forty-three years. It was discovered there was no evidence, there were no witnesses, and no DNA. The prosecuting attorney was fired, shortly after the man's conviction, due to implementing shady strategies to win cases.

In Winston-Salem, North Carolina, in 1984, a man was wrongfully convicted of murder. He was not released when DNA proved him innocent in 1994, but in 2004. It took ten years of appeals to exonerate him (innocenceproject.org).

In Buffalo, New York, in 1987, a man was wrongfully convicted as the "bike path rapist" (innocenceproject.org). He was finally released in 2007 after DNA testing exonerated him. Starting in 1997, he stood in front of the parole board every other year, but he could not be considered for parole unless he admitted guilt. Even though the bike path rapes *continued after he was imprisoned*, the evidence that would have exonerated him remained in a drawer at the medical center for twenty years.

Think about how often we are absolutely 100 percent sure of what we saw or know. Eyewitness error is the highest cause for a wrongful conviction at the rate of 75 percent (public.psych.iastate.edu).

There are numerous cases like these in our country and around the world.

Organizations like the **Innocence Project**, **Seeking Justice for the Innocent**, Oregon-based newspaper the **US Observer**, and others, have dedicated themselves to exonerating the wrongly convicted. Give these organizations a look, maybe you can help. Many law-abiding, decent citizens, just like you and me, are behind bars as we speak.

Get informed. Get involved.

I lost a lot of sleep the week I researched this topic.

It makes a person seriously rethink the death penalty. If this thought has not crossed your mind as you're reading this, you might want to re-examine your ideas.

Overpopulation

People have all sorts of beliefs and reasons for having large families. Imagine for a moment the millions of different opinions on how many children people should or should not have.

But what do opinions and personal belief matter when overpopulation, pollution, and clean water availability are in a state of disaster worldwide and getting worse every day.

Some people are saying disconnected things like, "So what, I can afford to have a big family."

These people behave as if their children live in another universe, not drinking water from the same water tables, not using the same resources, and not eating from the same crops.

If you believe that this subject does not concern you, consider that there is no magic space between major bodies of water. Just as there is no magic space between the atmosphere and different nations. That line you see when you look at a map is just a line on the map. Don't kid yourself. **Everything is connected.** And everything will have a profound impact on all of us.

The planet's cup runneth over with hungry mouths, dry fields, and dead bodies. Can your bank account cover *that*?

Recycling

Recycling might seem trivial in the big scheme of things, but it *does* make a difference. In some cases, a big difference. It is not just about rinsing cans and returning bottles. Recycling comes in many innovative forms.

Yard sales. Hand-me-downs. Restoration of old cars. Utilizing wood from old structures. Reusing well-preserved material from old curtains and couches to make unique fabrics.

I have heard arguments against recycling because items must be rinsed, which wastes water. I hear what they are saying, but if we can take forty-five-minute showers, have water parks, tolerate sprinklers watering sidewalks, wash six loads of laundry a week because we have too many clothes, and we have enough water for fracking—I can only conclude that we can use water for recycling. There is some gray area here, but it does not change the basic truth and its premise.

I heard a comedian making fun of recycling. He said how dumb we were to think that reusing products worked because it "Costs money to recycle." Yes, money is a headache for most of the world. And *when you can't feed your own children, you're probably not thinking about where the garbage is going. However, in the **industrialized world**, in the **free world**, in our world, **we have education, opportunities**, and **choices**. Most of us know about landfills.*

We know that stuff we throw away takes up room. One does not need a doctorate in space and time to understand that if we move our old couch from here, it will end up over there. It has to go somewhere. Someone's county. Someone's favorite, outdoor spot. Someone's neighborhood. Maybe mine. Maybe yours.

If we're only thinking of recycling in terms of money, then we are more ignorant than the illiterate guy living in a hole. At least he is not likely making a ton of garbage.

Maybe we *are* all screwed, and it will make no difference in the long run, but I would prefer to keep acting as if I am still alive and my life and actions *do* matter.

Money comes and goes. Space on Earth does not.

Talk about cost.

Planetary Warmth

Let's list what we know. It's a short list.

We know the planet has its own patterns, which have nothing to do with man. We know that humans measure the physical world via science. We know that according to our science, mankind is making its own substantial contribution to the damage and imbalance in our physical world.

A disturbing example of the damage we are incurring is the Texas-sized Trash Patch in the Pacific Ocean (education.nationalgeographic.com). I am *not* here to argue whether garbage causes global warming. What I *am* saying is that if you're not troubled by a state-sized spread of garbage, you might be in a coma. The point is, we are definitely causing serious harm to our environment and to our future on this planet, and in a variety of ways.

I know our public servants have lied to us for so long that we don't know what to believe, but for a moment let's be practical. Let's leave the arguing aside and ask: **"What can we do to slow down *our* contribution to the *current* SPEED of planetary changes?"**

Corporations are doing everything in their power to have us on their side. How else will they secure their lavish lifestyles and power? Greed is deadening to our human hearts. It is manipulative and deceitful. It is full of bonuses and handshakes of approval. Simple powers of observation and humanity held hostage by politics, padded wallets, and country clubs.

Is it God's will? I can only speak for myself, but fear of death and not seeing my loved ones again is powerful and traumatizing indeed. Due to my own heart-numbing fears, I understand why so many hold on to the idea that what's happening is about prophecy, as if holding on to dear life.

Ultimately all of us live on this planet *now.* Why would any of us – regardless of what we believe, not want to take care of our home? This is what doesn't make sense. After all, we're all in the same sinking boat, yet we're not arguing about how to slow the spiral down; but whether it's sinking.

You wouldn't leave a hole in your roof after a storm because the storm wasn't man-made or let someone take a jackhammer to your kitchen *today* because you know you're going to die *someday.* Would you?

There are places in this world where a woman would be killed for showing her elbows in public.

There are places in this world that would think it strange for a woman to go out of her way to hide her elbows in public.

Both beliefs are cultural, and 100 percent learned. Culture is acquired knowledge, not something we are born with.

It is important to point out that elbows are a basic component of arms, which are used to open doors, pick up babies, and eat.

No one is born with a powerful, driving, natural force, to instinctively want to show or hide one's elbows.

But when we are confronted by a cheat, a backstabber, a gossiper, a malicious tongue, a charlatan, a cold-blooded killer, an aggressor, a vile or a grossly selfish person, we cross political and cultural boundaries. No matter where we are from, we know deep down that these things have no honor and are depraved. No matter what we were taught, it is something we innately feel.

These are the binds between us that break us and make us—not as a culture, a flag, a social norm, or a religious belief, but as a human race.

Simple truths of right and wrong cross all borders. Anything outside of that simplicity is cultural make-believe.

Think of the suffering this type of indoctrination has caused our world. Think of the suffering it has caused you and your loved ones. Start recognizing the difference as soon as you possibly can.

Now would be good.

We hold onto our externally programmed ideas and fantasies, no matter how common, wonderful, or absurd, even when they are past serving their purpose. We hold on to them as though they are a life-vest in the frigid waters of the ocean—but maybe we need to drown.

Maybe only then we can be reborn, not as someone new but as our true selves. Unveiled, discovered, unabridged, and with miraculous possibilities. Connected. Sober. Cleaner. More aware. Fighting with vengeance for humanity, love, and a better life.

It is these rare, courageous, and compassionate humans who show up and somehow manage to get through the thick skin of indoctrination. They reveal themselves to live as they were meant to be. They think for themselves, and with clarity they fend-off the societal dirt that sticks to the masses. They take leaps and bounds and, as a side effect, they infuse others with inspiration.

And all of that because they have the foresight to figure out who they are, and the courage to do the irreplaceable, one-of-a-kind thing only they can do.

When the moment comes and you lay on your deathbed, will you say, "I was not bitter enough?" Or will you be washed over with a late realization? And in vain try to mouth the words with your tired lips, "I did not love enough. Create enough. Forgive enough. Laugh enough. It went by in a blink of an eye."

There is a bit of Mother Teresa, Galileo, Mandela, Helen Keller, Emil Kapaun, Gandhi, Harriet Tubman, Tesla, Martin Luther King, Luis Martins de Souza Dantas, Abe Lincoln, and Harriet Beecher Stowe, in all of us.

Start your own ripple effect.

Ragnar: "So have you returned to your faith, renounced ours?"
Athelstan: "I wish it was so simple. In the gentle fall of rain from
Heaven, I hear my God. But in the thunder, I
still hear Thor. That is my agony."
Ragnar: "I hope that someday our Gods can become friends."
– *Vikings*

"When I heard the learn'd astronomer;
When the proofs, the figures, were ranged in columns before me;
when I was shown the charts and the diagrams, to add, divide and
measure them;
When I, sitting, heard the astronomer, where he lectured
with much applause in the lecture room,
How soon, unaccountable, I became tired and sick;
Till rising and gliding out, I wander'd off by myself,
In the mystical moist night-air, and from time to time,
Look'd up in perfect silence at the stars."

– Walt Whitman

About the Author

Although the author was raised in a stressful and at times harsh environment, she had the good fortune to grow up in a home with a courageous mother and a caring extended family. Literacy, music, affection, and a combination of science and faith were present in her everyday life. Her curiosity about nature, justice, and civilizations led her to love libraries and the history within them. She resides with her family in the Pacific Northwest.